KEVIN PIETERSEN

ENGLAND CRICKETER

MR VIVEK KUMAR PANDEY

Made with ♥ on the Notion Press Platform
www.notionpress.com

Contents

Foreword

Short Biography Of Kevin Pietersen & Life Style, Career etc. During Writing This Book No Character, No Religion & No Caste Are Harmed. It's Only For Study Purpose. We don't want to hurt anyone.

Preface

Author biography in English :

MY NAME IS VIVEK KUMAR PANDEY . I WAS BORN IN 30 SEP 2002,I AM FROM SURAT GUJARAT INDIA.MY DREAM WAS TO BE GOOD WRITERS ,MY FAMILY SUPPORTED ME TO SUCCESSFUL AND I CAN DO IT MY SELF.How do I write? That is a question, I believe, that can be honestly answered by me."CELEBRATING YOUNGEST WRITER AWARD WINNER IN GUJARAT 1ST RANK" MR PANDEY JI . I may think I did a good job writing something. The reader is the one who decides the quality of my writing. I do find writing to be natural to me and therefore find it to be a real challenge. My trick as a challenged writer is to do the best I can and know that I am happy with the final outcome. It may take a while to do my best and there may be quite a few problems I run into along the way.

I am not a greedy person those who are thinking about me and my self I never tried it anyone people suffering from sadness ,I trying to get promoted people suffering from happiness and joy in your Life Time. Now in current situation in India and also world people are unemployed and have no many but our indian governor help to people to get free food from ration card , i also take part in leadership team ,i am Motivational speaker , Film script writer. There was my two dream firstly writer and secondly actor & also my own film is upcoming soon i done almost completely completed script for my film .I AM GOING TO SAY WORD OF HEART TOUCH OUT PLEASE READ IT" , firstly i thanks my father he supports me in this field they always getting inspired me by own his words and behavior ,they always said that he was a biggest person in the world in future and also they purchase fruit and chocolate for me in anytime & anyway , firstly my father buy him then call me Vivek you want a chocolate i will say yes papa but how many tell me ,papa: you tell me how much i buy him i told 1 or 2 chocolate but my father purchase whole the boxes of chocolate and they get suprised me. MY FATHER WAS BORN IN " 20 SEPTEMBER" 1971 IN INDIA.

1) MY FATHER FAVORITE CLOTHES IS KURTA PAIJMA AND ALSO STYLES SHOE

2) FAVORITE SINGER IS KISHORE DA

3) FAVORITE STATE GUJARAT AND KOLKATA , HIS VILLAGE IN BIHAR

4) FAVORITE COLOR BLACK AND WHITE

THEY ALSO LOVE cricket like IPL and one day t-20 .they also like watching a News daily and heard the song daily ,they also interested in tik tok video but in current time tik tok is banned in india but also few videos are in you tube. In lockdown time my family and me very enjoy day daily. my father play daily ludo with his sister and son, daughter.they always loved tea and coffee anytime call me . I make it tea for my father but some reason after the April to june they are suffering from fever and cough , weakness on 6 June 2020 my father death. they not told me say bye bye his life. After death of 6 June on 10 june my mom and dad anniversary.but my father is Best in the world they can do anything for me please take care of father and respect it of your parents.

ONE

KEVIN PIETERSEN

- **Kevin Pietersen**

1. Short Biography Of Kevin Pietersen & Life Style, Career etc. During Writing This Book No Character, No Religion & No Caste Are Harmed. It's Only For Study Purpose. We don't want to hurt anyone.

Kevin Pietersen (born 27 June 1980) is a cricket commentator, conservationist, and former England international cricket player. He is a right-handed batsman and occasional off spin bowler who played in all three formats for England between 2005 and 2014, which included a brief tenure as captain.

Pietersen was born to an Afrikaner father and English mother in South Africa. He made his first-class debut for Natal in 1997 and moved to England in 2000, after voicing his displeasure at what he said was the racial quota system in South African cricket. Being of English ancestry, Pietersen was eligible for the England team so long as he first served a four-year qualifying period in English county cricket. He was called up by England almost immediately after he completed four years with Nottinghamshire. He made his international debut in the One Day International (ODI) match against Zimbabwe in 2004 and his Test match debut in the 2005 Ashes series against Australia.

Pietersen left Nottinghamshire for Hampshire in 2005, but the England team's subsequent reliance on him resulted in Pietersen making only a single first-class appearance for his new county between 2005 and 2010. In June 2010, Pietersen announced his wish to leave Hampshire. he joined Surrey on loan for the remainder of the season, then moved permanently in 2011.

Pietersen was captain of the England Test and ODI teams from 4 August 2008 to 7 January 2009, but resigned after just three Tests and nine ODIs following a dispute with the England coach Peter Moores, who was sacked the same day. Pietersen's relationship with the ECB never fully recovered. This came to a head in 2012 when, after a disagreement over his schedule, Pietersen announced his retirement from all forms of international limited-overs cricket on 31 May. Although he later retracted his retirement, his relationship with both the ECB and his team-mates soured during the series against South Africa, and he was dropped for the final Test of that series. Pietersen last played for England in the 2013–14 Ashes and subsequent ODIs, after which he was informed that he was no longer being considered for international selection.

He also played for the Melbourne Stars in the Big Bash League until the end of BBL|07 (seventh season), the Quetta Gladiators in the Pakistan Super League as well as the Hollywoodbets Dolphins in the CSA T20 Challenge. He was also signed by the Rising Pune Supergiants for the 2016 season of the Indian Premier League.

Pietersen is one of the fastest batsman to reach 1,000 ODI runs and still holds the record for being the fastest player to cross 2,000 runs in One Day International cricket. He has the second-highest run total from his first 25 Tests, behind only Sir Don Bradman of Australia, and was the fastest player, in terms of days, to reach 4,000, 5,000 and 7,000 Test runs. He became only the third English batsman to top the ICC One Day International rankings, doing so in March 2007. In July 2008, after a century against South Africa, The Times called him "the most complete batsman in cricket" and in 2012 The Guardian called him "England's greatest modern batsman". On the occasion of England's 1000th Test in August 2018, he was named in the country's greatest Test XI by the ECB. He won the Player of the Series award for his heroics in 2010 ICC World Twenty20 and for helping the England Cricket Team win their maiden ICC trophy.

- **Kevin Pietersen personal life**

Pietersen had a strict and disciplined childhood, along with his three brothers Tony, Greg and Bryan; he learned valuable lessons from this "fantastic" approach to parenting, and said: "Discipline is good. It taught me that I didn't always have to have what I wanted; that what I needed was different from what I wanted." Bryan played club and second XI cricket in England. A forearm injury at 11 years old meant Pietersen could not play rugby, but he played hockey, tennis and squash, which also made his right arm very strong for batting.

Pietersen attended Maritzburg College, Pietermaritzburg, and made his first-class cricket debut for Natal's B team in 1997, aged 17, where he was regarded predominantly as an off spin bowler and a hard-hitting lower-order batsman. After two seasons, he moved to England for a five-month spell as the overseas player for club side Cannock CC, helping them win the Birmingham and District Premier League in 2000. This first spell away from home did not leave him with fond memories for England, in particular "those horrible Black Country accents" referring to a dialect of the West Midlands, living in a single room above a squash court, and working in the club bar. However, he returned to newly renamed KwaZulu Natal side a better cricketer; a lack of opportunities to bowl had improved his batting.

Having seen Pietersen play at a school cricket festival, Clive Rice invited him to sign for Nottinghamshire County Cricket Club. Pietersen accepted without hesitation, keen to make the most of top-class cricket under a coach for whom he had the utmost admiration. He did not at this stage contemplate forsaking his nation; it had not yet occurred to him that the decision would have to be taken.

Pietersen is widely portrayed in the media as having a self-assured personality, described by Geoffrey Boycott as being "cocky and confident". Former England test captain Michael Vaughan counters this, saying, "KP is not a confident person. He obviously has great belief in his ability but that's not quite the same thing... And I know KP wants to be loved. I try to text him and talk to him as often as I can because I know he is insecure." He has been noted for unusual haircuts, with his peroxide blonde-dyed streak of hair along the middle of his head during the 2005 Ashes series being described as a "dead skunk" look. During the 2006–07 Ashes tour, the Australian team, noted for their efforts to dominate opponents psychologically, dubbed him "The Ego", or "FIGJAM" (Fuck I'm Good, Just Ask Me). Other nicknames include "KP", "Kelves" and "Kapes".

Pietersen is married to former Liberty X singer Jessica Taylor. The couple married on 29 December 2007 at St Andrew's Church in Castle Combe, Wiltshire, with former England team-mate Darren Gough acting as best man.

Jessica gave birth to the couple's first child, a son, in 2010. Pietersen travelled back from touring with the England side in Barbados to be present at the birth. He arrived at the hospital just in time for the birth. Their second child, a daughter, was born in 2015. Pietersen took leave from playing for the Melbourne Stars in the Big Bash League in Australia to be present for the birth.Pietersen considers South Africa his first home and England his second home, and the family split their time between Surrey and the Sabie River.

- **Kevin Pietersen Domestic career**

He impressed members of Nasser Hussain's England side when playing for KwaZulu Natal in 1999; he took four top-order wickets and, despite batting at number nine, scored 61 not out from 57 balls, hitting four sixes. Hussain then recommended that Pietersen secure a contract with an English county side.

Despite the praise from the England side, Pietersen claimed he was dropped from the Natal first team. Pietersen felt that this was due to the country's racial quota system, in which provincial sides were required to have at least four black players. Pietersen's view was that players should be judged on merit, and described it as "heartbreaking" when he was left out of the side, although he later reflected "it turned out it was the best thing that could have happened". However, in the 1999-2000 Supersport series, from four matches Pietersen only averaged 10.75 with the bat, and took 10 wickets at an expensive 37.50, which were not enough to cement his place in the KwaZulu Natal side. Nonetheless, Pietersen has since firmly criticised the quota system, which he feels forced him out of the country of his birth.

He has also criticised Graeme Smith, who became captain of the South African side in 2003, calling him "an absolute muppet, childish and strange" and that his behaviour "leaves a lot to be desired". Smith opposed this, saying, "I'm patriotic about my country, and that's why I don't like Kevin Pietersen. The only reason that Kevin and I have never had a relationship is because he slated South Africa". Pietersen's outspoken views published in his autobiography, Crossing the Boundary, in September 2006, and in an interview for the South African edition of GQ magazine, led to unsuccessful calls for an ICC investigation regarding bringing the game into disrepute.

- **Kevin Pietersen English domestic career**

In 2000, Nottinghamshire coach Clive Rice, who had seen Pietersen play in 1997 in South Africa at a schools week, heard that Pietersen was playing club cricket for the Cannock Cricket Club and offered him a three-year contract to play for the county. His maiden first-class century came on his Nottinghamshire debut against Loughborough UCCE. In his first season, he made 1,275 runs with an impressive batting average of 57.95, including 218 not out in an unbroken sixth-wicket stand of 352 with John Morris at Derby in July, after having been out lbw for a duck in the first innings.These performances led to praise in the Wisden Cricketers' Almanack: "If he can maintain his first season's form, the name of Pietersen should be pencilled in for future Test squads."This form did indeed continue into the following year: he made another unbeaten double-century, against Middlesex, taking part in a partnership of 316 for the fourth wicket with Darren Bicknell. This period proved to be a purple patch for the batsman, scoring four consecutive centuries (254 not out, 122, 147 and 116) in one week in August.

In 2003, Pietersen scored 1,546 first-class runs, and 764 runs in limited overs cricket. He was selected for the 2003/04 ECB National Academy tour of India, and had a successful tour scoring 523 runs including three centuries in his six first-class innings to record an average of 104.60, and making 131 in a one-day match against India A in Bangalore.

After Nottinghamshire were relegated in 2003, Pietersen requested a release from his contract, saying "I haven't been happy for a while....The pitch at Trent Bridge has been one of my problems... I could have done so much better if the wicket had been good."This led to a public row with club captain Jason Gallian, where Gallian allegedly threw Pietersen's kit off the Trent Bridge balcony and broke his bat:

During the game I told the captain that I was not happy and that I wanted to leave. After the game we spoke in the dressing room and then I went to have dinner. I got a call saying the captain had trashed my equipment. I was told the captain had said, 'if he does not want to play for Notts he can f*** off.' I have not spoken to Gallian since, nor have I received an apology.Pietersen was made to honour the last year of his contract at Nottinghamshire, but "didn't enjoy it at all".

In October 2004, he joined Hampshire under the captaincy of Shane Warne. After becoming a regular in the national side, Pietersen rarely got an opportunity to play domestic cricket. Having an England "central contract" meant that Pietersen was only released to play for Hampshire at the discretion of the national coach. After being left out of the national side to face Bangladesh in May 2005, Pietersen had several good innings in the English County Championship, including two centuries. He only played twice for the county in 2006, and appeared just once in 2007, with an unbeaten 66 against Ireland. Pietersen's last first-class match for Hampshire came in the 2008 County Championship against Somerset, where he scored 100 runs in Hampshire's first innings, and following the birth of his son, a desire to stay in London led to him announcing he would leave Hampshire at the end of the 2010 season.

Pietersen then joined Surrey on loan from Hampshire for the remainder of the 2010 English county cricket season. He scored a century in his first Clydesdale Bank 40 appearance against Sussex, with 116 off 105 deliveries. It was his first limited overs century since 2008, and his first century of any kind since March 2009. He subsequently signed permanently for Surrey from the 2011 season onwards. Pietersen had also rejoined his old team in South Africa, the Dolphins, for a short stint in October 2010.

In early 2015, Pietersen withdrew from the initial stages of the 2015 Indian Premier League, instead opting to play County Championship matches, with the aim of playing for England again. After a meeting with Andrew Strauss, the new Director of Cricket for England, whilst not out on 326 overnight against Leicestershire, during which Strauss rejected any notions of a return for Pietersen, Pietersen resumed his innings the following day, scoring his highest first-class score of 355*.

On 19 July 2017 Pietersen returned to English domestic cricket when he joined Surrey for the NatWest t20 Blast. He scored 52 runs, including four consecutive sixes. He was replaced by a substitute fielder in the second innings. On 29 July Pietersen announced that he had decided to donate all his earnings towards rhino conservation efforts. After being injured for the majority of the season, making only one further T20 appearance, Pietersen announced that he would leave Surrey, and English cricket as a whole, following the club's loss in the quarter finals to Birmingham Bears.

- **Kevin Pietersen in Indian Premier League**

In February 2014, Delhi Daredevils of Indian Premier League bought Pietersen for US$1.5 million for the 2014 Indian Premier League season, and he captained the team for that season. Pietersen had previously played for the Delhi Daredevils during the 2012 Indian Premier League Season and had his most successful IPL season by scoring 305 runs at a strike rate of 147, which included a victorious knock of 103*.

In the 2015 Indian Premier League auction, Pietersen was bought by Sunrisers Hyderabad for 2 Crore Rupees. However, Pietersen was released by Sunrisers Hyderabad prior to the start of the tournament, although he could play in the later stages of the 2015 Indian Premier League season. Plans to rejoin Hyderabad towards the end of the competition were curtailed due to injury.

- **Kevin Pietersen as Melbourne Stars**

Pietersen was signed by the Melbourne Stars in 2014–15 Big Bash League season, with a contract for 2 years. he was seen as a "big hit" for the 2014–15 Big Bash League season. On 18 December 2014, Kevin Pietersen played his first match in 2014–15 Big Bash League season as the no.3 batsmen, and scored 66 runs off 46 balls. In 2016, he helped the team beat two-time defending champion Perth Scorchers and advance to their first Grand Final and their fifth consecutive Finals series appearances. Pietersen also signed a two-year extension that took him through to the 2017–18 season.

- **Kevin Pietersen International career**

Pietersen is eligible to play for England as he has an English mother. After a qualifying period of four years playing at English county level, he was called up almost immediately for his international debut against Zimbabwe in 2004.

The tour of Zimbabwe caused several players to voice their concerns about the Robert Mugabe regime, the security issues in the country and the standard of the Zimbabwean side. Steve Harmison was the first to boycott the tour for "political and sporting reasons", and all-rounder Andrew Flintoff was reported to be considering taking a moral stand himself. The England Chairman of Selectors David Graveney denied that the selectors would leave out players unhappy with touring Zimbabwe and would put their absences down to injury. Flintoff was, however, "rested" and Pietersen rushed into the squad "at the earliest opportunity". In the five match ODI series, Pietersen batted in three innings which included a score of 77 not out; he finished the series with an average of 104.00 as England won the series 4–0.

- **Success in South Africa**

Pietersen was upset not to be initially in the squad to tour South Africa. With Flintoff withdrawing due to injury, Pietersen was recalled to the squad, and cemented his place in the first team with 97 off 84 balls in the warm-up match against South Africa A, in the face of a hostile crowd. Throughout the tour, Pietersen was subjected to a barrage of abuse from the South African crowd, who regarded him somewhat like a traitor. He said: I knew I was going to cop a lot of stick but it will be like water off a duck's back...I expected stick at the start of the innings, and I'm sure it will carry on through the whole series. But I just sat back and laughed at the opposition, with their swearing and 'traitor' remarks... some of them can hardly speak English. My affiliation is with England. In fact, I'm starting to speak too much like Darren Gough... In fact, I'm going to get one of Gough's tattoos with three lions and my number underneath...No one can say I'm not English.

Pietersen scored a 96-ball 108 not out in the tied second ODI at Bloemfontein, after which the crowd turned their backs on him as he returned to the pavilion. This score set his ODI average at an incredible record 234.00. He made 75 at Cape Town, then at East London Pietersen made an unbeaten 100 from only 69 balls, the fastest century by an England player in a one-day match, although England still lost by eight runs. In the final game at Centurion Park, Pietersen came to the wicket at 32/3 and scored 116, but again could not prevent a defeat. Pietersen ended the series, which England lost 4–1, with 454 runs in five innings, and the Player of the Series award. By the end of the series, the South African crowds had generally replaced hostility with respect for Pietersen, his final century being awarded a standing ovation.

Despite press speculation, Pietersen was not picked for the Tests against Bangladesh—his early season form being dogged by a foot injury but with his county form improving, he was selected for the Twenty20 match against Australia at Southampton, making 34 from 18 balls and taking three catches as England won by 100 runs. He was awarded 'man of the match'.

In the triangular ODI series against Australia and Bangladesh, Pietersen did not get to bat in the first match at The Oval as England won by 10 wickets, but scored 91 off 65 balls in the match in Bristol against Australia. In the remainder of the triangular series, Pietersen scored quickly, although without other half-centuries. In the final of the NatWest Series, he only made 6 as he finished the seven-match series with a total of 278 runs at an average of 46.33.

Pietersen's performances sparked speculation over whether he would be brought into the Test side for The Ashes later in the summer. Later in July, Pietersen played in all three matches of the (ODI) NatWest Challenge against Australia. In the final match he was the top scorer for England with 74 runs; however, he was forced off the field in the third over of Australia's reply with a groin injury.

- **Kevin Pietersen in 2005 Ashes triumph**

Speculation over when Pietersen would play for the Test team was ended in July with the announcement by the England chairman of selectors, David Graveney, that Pietersen had been selected ahead of Graham Thorpe. He made his debut in the first Ashes Test at Lord's, becoming the 626th player to play for the national side. He came into bat at 18–3 and he made 57 on debut in his first innings. In the second innings, he similarly came in after a batting collapse and finished making a second half-century and finished the innings on 64 not out, becoming only the fourth player to top score in both innings on debut for England, the eighth England player to score a half-century in each innings on his debut, and the third cricketer to do so at Lord's.

England were thrashed by 239 runs before moving onto Edgbaston where he came in a more comfortable position scoring 71 in the first innings. He had a good partnership with Andrew Flintoff where the pair put on 103 very quickly. He made 20 in the second innings coming in at 31–4. He was involved in two controversial decisions: he gloved his first ball from Brett Lee, but the umpire turned down the appeal, and he was later given out to a ball from Shane Warne that hit his pad then elbow before being caught by Adam Gilchrist. England won the match by two runs.

In the drawn third Test, Pietersen had his first quiet match when he scored 21 in the first innings, getting caught on the boundary. Then, with England looking to push on he was dismissed lbw by Glenn McGrath for a golden duck. In the fourth test, at his former home ground Trent Bridge, he scored 45 in the first innings after facing 108 balls looking to build a big score. In the second innings chasing 129 to win, he was in at 57–4 when he scored 23 in a decent partnership again with Flintoff. He was dismissed when he was caught behind wafting at a ball outside off stump. However, England won and went 2–1 up.

Under pressure to post a large score in the final Test at The Oval, Pietersen did not contribute significantly in the first innings; he scored 14 as he was bowled by Shane Warne for the first time in his Test career . In the second innings, Pietersen was dropped on 0 by a combination of Gilchrist and Hayden, on 15 by his Hampshire colleague Shane Warne and after reaching fifty on 60 by Shaun Tait. He reached his maiden test century with a driven four off the bowling of Tait before making 158, eventually being dismissed by Glenn McGrath. This innings helped to secure the return of the Ashes to England. His innings included seven sixes, breaking Ian Botham's record for the most sixes by an English player in an Ashes innings.

Pietersen was named Man of the Match for his efforts, and finished the series as top scorer, with 473 runs over the five Tests, an average of 52.55, which also was the highest in the series. However, he had a less successful series in the field, dropping six catches in the five Tests, a point he made wryly when questioned about the Australians dropping him three times on the final day. Pietersen was given an ECB central contract to reflect his place in the national side.

- **Kevin Pietersen in 2005–06 winter tour**

Pietersen had a less successful time in the three Test matches against Pakistan, which England lost 2–0. He made little impact in the first and third test. His first Test match innings since his match winning 158 against Australia was brief as he was caught at short leg for 5. In the second innings, he was criticised for his dismissal. Chasing just 198, he was caught behind after a horrible slog on 19 as England went on to lose by 22 runs. In the third test, he made 34 before edging behind in the first innings. With England in difficulty, Pietersen edged Danish Kaneria to short leg when only on one, as England were to be defeated by an innings.

He fared better in the second, however, making his second Test century in the first innings. He brought up his hundred with a six before next ball, he top-edged a pull and was out. In the next innings, with England needing to bat out a draw, England were 20–4 but he made 42 to help England get the draw. He was also performing well in the one-day series with two explosive innings of 56 from 39 balls to help England win the first ODI, and 28 from 27 balls in the second. The quick-scoring innings in the second ODI was to be Pietersen's last on the tour. A rib injury sustained in the first ODI proved too painful throughout the second, and Pietersen returned to England to recover fully for the tour of India.

In March 2006, Pietersen played in the three Tests against India, which England drew 1–1. In the first innings on 15, another rash shot brought his downfall. He pulled a ball from Sreesanth onto his stumps. His 87 in the second innings of the first match came during England's acceleration period, helping push the required target over 300.

England then declared overnight, and India successfully batted out the final day to secure a draw. This half-century was followed by another in the first innings of the second Test. Again, he gave his wicket away on 64 when he offered Munaf Patel a return catch. The second innings was not so good, facing just 13 balls before being given out caught behind off a Harbhajan Singh delivery. The unhappy Pietersen was later fined 30 percent of his match fee for shaking his head and showing signs of dissent. Replays demonstrated that the ball that had dismissed him had brushed his forearm, not his glove, before ballooning up into the hands of Rahul Dravid at slip. But umpire Darrell Hair gave him out for 4 as England collapsed on the fourth afternoon.

Pietersen posted a score of 39 in the first innings of the third test before he got a beauty from Sreesanth which moved and took the edge of the bat before being caught by Mahendra Singh Dhoni. In the second innings, he posted 7 again being caught and bowled, this time by Anil Kumble via a leading edge. Despite a quiet match for him, England won comfortably after a dismal 100 all out in India's second visit to the crease.In the one-day series, which England lost 5–1, he was top scorer for England in four out of the five matches he played, and had the highest average of any player with 58.20. His 71 in the second ODI took him past 1,000 ODI runs, equalling Viv Richards' record of 21 innings to reach this total.

- **Sri Lanka and Pakistan in England, 2006**

In May 2006, Pietersen matched his highest Test score of 158 in the first match against Sri Lanka. His innings was ended when he was lbw to Chaminda Vaas. In the second test he made 142 at Edgbaston. He made almost half of England's runs. After he made his hundred, his third six saw the introduction to the Switch hit, when he turned out and played a switch hit sweep off Muttiah Muralitharan. This took him past the milestone of 1,000 Test runs, in his 12th Test match, and he became the first batsman since Graham Gooch in 1990 to score a century in three successive Test innings on English soil. This performance moved Pietersen into the top ten of the ICC cricket ratings. In the third test, he was twice removed by Murali. In the first innings, on 41, he top edged a sweep to short fine leg. In the second innings with England chasing 325, he was caught at short leg for just 6. Despite this, his performances in the first two tests earned him the England (Test match) Player of the Series.

In the first and second tests of the Pakistan series, he got starts with the bat but did not get past 50. He was out lbw, offering no shot, in the first innings at Lords for 21. In the second innings, when England were pushing on, he played some nice strokes in his 41 before being stumped of the bowling of Shahid Afridi. In the second test, he made 38 when he hit a half-volley loosely to point. In the third Test at Headingley, he hit 135 runs from England's total of 515. In the final controversial test at The Oval, on a horribly wet pitch, he got the second golden duck of his Test career when he edged behind. In the second innings, he made 96 before edging behind again before the test came to an unexpected early end.

- **Asif bowls Pietersen for a duck**

Pietersen bowled his first delivery in Test match cricket on 4 June, against Sri Lanka. His first Test wicket came against Pakistan later in the summer when Kamran Akmal got a thin edge through to Geraint Jones. Later in June, Pietersen scored 17 in the Twenty20 International as England lost by 2 runs to Sri Lanka. The twenty over match against Pakistan was no better, Pietersen being bowled by Mohammad Asif for a golden duck as Pakistan helped themselves to a five-wicket victory.

- **England in Australia, 2006–07**

In the much-anticipated Ashes series in Australia, Pietersen was hyped up as England's best player and this was justified as he scored 490 runs in five matches and averaged over fifty, despite Australia's obvious targeting of him. "I was interested to see how he would get on in Australia in 2006–07 on pitches with more bounce", wrote Warne, "because bowlers had tried to test him with the short ball. He was still England's best batsman."

He started well, in the First Test. Despite a failure of 16 in the first test, he produced a fine spell of batting with a good 92 in the second innings. This wasn't enough to save England from a 277 run defeat. In the second Test, he backed up his good form with a century in the Second Test in Adelaide, sharing a 310-run partnership for the fourth wicket with Paul Collingwood. When he was eventually run out, his first reaction was to "giggle" because it was the third time in his Test career that he had scored exactly 158 runs, which was, at that point, his highest Test score. However, he made 2 in a disastrous second innings collapse which cost England dear. In the third test, he was the only batsman to offer any resistance with 70 in the first innings and 60 not out in the second innings in a defeat which cost England the Ashes. However, he couldn't carry on that form as he failed to make a half-century in the final two tests as England lost 5–0.

Pietersen bowling off-spin in the Adelaide Oval nets in November 2006.In the tour's sole Twenty20 match, Pietersen was run out on eleven as England lost by 77 runs. In the first One Day International of the 2006–07 Commonwealth Bank Series, on 12 January at the Melbourne Cricket Ground, Pietersen was injured when a ball bowled by Glenn McGrath hit him on the ribs. Despite continuing his innings in some discomfort, making 82, X-rays revealed a fracture, and Pietersen was forced to miss the rest of the series.

- **Kevin Pietersen in 2007 Cricket World Cup**

In the 2007 Cricket World Cup, England started in Group C with a game against New Zealand in which KP made 60 before holing out. He made another 50 against Kenya but disappointedly made just 5 against Canada as England sealed qualification. He made 48 in the unconvincing win against Ireland. Pietersen made 58 against Sri Lanka before being caught and bowled by Murali. England lost that game by 2 runs before losing the next game against Australia by 7 wickets. Pietersen crafted 104 runs off 122 balls against Australia. It was the first World Cup century by an Englishman since 1996, and the first ever against Australia.

His efforts in the World Cup helped him achieve the status of International Cricket Council number-one ranked batsman in the world for ODIs. He then failed making 10 against Bangladesh and 3 against South Africa. England lost to South Africa meaning that England did not reach the semi-finals. In England's final match of the World Cup against the West Indies, Pietersen made 100 from 91 balls, and effected the run-out of retiring captain Brian Lara. This century took him past 2,000 ODI runs, in doing so equalling the record 51 matches set by Zaheer Abbas. He finished the tournament with 444 runs, at an average of 55.5, and was described as shining in the England team "like a 100 watt bulb in a room full of candles". He was named in the 'Team of the Tournament' by Cricinfo.

- **West Indies in England**

In the first test of the series he was dismissed for 26 again chasing a wide one when looking set also after 4 centuries were scored by England batsmen in the innings at Lord's, he then scored a hundred in the second innings when England were looking to accelerate.Pietersen posted his highest score of 226 in the second Test at Headingley (it was scored in 262 balls, with 24 fours and 2 sixes), surpassing his previous best of 158 which he had achieved three times. With this score, Pietersen moved ahead of Everton Weekes and Viv Richards to be the batsman with the second-highest run-total out of his first 25 Tests (behind Don Bradman). It is also the highest Test score for England since Graham Gooch scored 333 against India in 1990. This innings subjected the West Indies to an innings and 283 runs defeat, their largest against any team. Pietersen, the Man of the Match, said, "I believe the recipe for success is hard work. I've been criticised for throwing my wicket away, and I tried to make it count here".

In the third Test at Old Trafford, he carried on his bad run at the ground being bounced out twice for 9 and 68. In the second innings, Pietersen lost his wicket in a bizarre dismissal when West Indian all-rounder Dwayne Bravo delivered a bouncer which knocked Pietersen's helmet off his head and onto his stumps. He is only the fourth batsman in Test cricket to be dismissed "hit wicket" as a result of headgear falling onto the stumps. This score took him past the 8,500 first-class runs mark, and 2,500 runs in Test cricket. In the final match of the series, he registered his third duck of his Test career in the first innings and 28 in the second innings as England won the series 3–0.

In contrast, Pietersen's batting was poor in the following single innings matches; he scored a total of 77 runs in five matches (two Twenty20 and three ODI), recording a second-ball duck in the final ODI. He subsequently fell to second in the official One Day International batting rankings, behind Ricky Ponting. Pietersen himself commented that his lack of form was a result of "fatigue", and reiterated his calls for a less "hectic" match schedule.

- **India tour and Twenty20 Championship**

Pietersen batting during the second Test of India's tour of England in 2007.Pietersen played in the first Test against India and in the first innings, he made 37 but not without controversy. He edged the ball behind of Zaheer Khan to Dhoni. He walked, but after seeing replays on the screen, he walked back to the middle and the decision was overturned. Ironically, he was out shortly afterwards caught Dhoni, bowled Khan. In the second innings he was top scorer with a knock of 134 to set up a potential England victory. Pietersen described this as his best century, in very testing conditions.

In the second test, he was twice lbw to RP Singh for 13 and 19 in a defeat which subsequently cost them the series. After making 41 in the first innings, Pietersen scored his 10th Test century in the third and final Test at the Oval, helping England to draw the game with 101. In the one-day series that followed, he struggled at the start with a top score of 33 not out in the first five matches of the series. He scored two half-centuries in the final matches including 71 not out in the final match at Lord's, hitting the winning runs to give England the series.

Pietersen was also picked for and played in the Twenty20 Championship in South Africa. In England's first game against Zimbabwe on 13 September, Pietersen hit 79 runs off 37 balls, his highest Twenty20 score, including seven fours and four sixes (one of them being another switch-hit sweep for six) in an English total of 188–9. England won the match by 50 runs; however, this was to be Pietersen's largest contribution in the competition. He scored another 99 runs over four more matches, ending the series with an average of 35.60. He also scored the most England fours (17) and jointly held the record for the most England sixes (6) with Owais Shah. He also held the highest strike rate of any England batsman.

- **Kevin Pietersen Career in 2008**

On England's tour against New Zealand, Pietersen averaged 33.00 in the ODI series, with one score of 50 in the tied fourth match; England lost the series 3–1. He also made a top score of 43 in the first of two comfortable Twenty20 matches. Pietersen had a quiet first two Test matches, making little impression with the bat. He produced 42 and 6 as England collapsed in their second innings. In the next test, he fared little better making 31 and 17. However, in the first innings of the Napier Test he rescued England from a disastrous start of 4–3, guiding them to 259 with 129, his 11th Test century.

New Zealand then came to tour England and Pietersen again struggled in the first two Test matches, scoring 3 in the first match. He improved slightly in the second but only making 26 in the first innings and then running himself out on 42 having looked well set. He seemed to be struggling particularly against Daniel Vettori but he showed no signs of that as he struck a century in the third Test, forming a valuable partnership with Tim Ambrose, making a crucial 115. Pietersen hit a winning 42 not out in the Twenty20 match.

In the first ODI of the NatWest series, Pietersen hit two sixes by "switch-hitting" en route to 110 not out. While facing the bowling of medium pace Scott Styris, Pietersen turned his body around and switched hands (effectively batting as a left-hander) hitting two sixes over cover and long off. Because Pietersen not only reversed his hand position (as some batsman do while playing the reverse sweep), but changed his stance by rotating his body, these "switch-hit" shots were immediately followed by calls to outlaw them from the game. Although a similar shot was played when Pietersen reverse-swept Muttiah Muralitharan for six in Sri Lanka in 2006, in this case he switched hands and executed "the switch" before the ball was bowled.

Several commentators complained that because Pietersen changed from being a right-handed to a left-handed batsman as the bowler approached his delivery stride, he was gaining an unfair advantage. Gideon Haigh said that "A bowler must advise a batsman when he's changing direction, why should the batsmen not; given that where the bowler's aiming will depend on the placement of the off stump". Ian Healy seconded this by saying "It just should be outlawed straightaway. If you want to hit to one side of the field, you've got to do it in a cross fashion, and not swap the way you're facing or your grip. Otherwise you are going to start to allow the bowlers to go round the wicket, over the wicket, and keep swapping during their run-ups." Former fast-bowler Michael Holding argued "if the batsman can change from being right-handed to left-handed, there shouldn't be a problem with a bowler changing from being right-handed to left-handed, either, without having to tell the umpire, nor should he have to tell the umpire if he is going over or round the wicket."

"That's ridiculous, absolutely stupid. The reverse-sweep has been part of the game for however long. I am just fortunate that I am able to hit it a bit further. Everybody wants brand new ideas, new inventions and new shots. That is a new shot played today and people should be saying it's a new way to go. There are new things happening for cricket at the moment and people shouldn't be criticising it all the time."

Another citation for the shot being outlawed was that the possibility of being out LBW ("a player is out LBW if...the ball pitches in line between wicket and wicket or on the off side of the striker's wicket") is removed, as the off side become the leg side and vice versa. The shots were considered by the Marylebone Cricket Club (MCC), governors of the game, who came to the conclusion that the shot was legal, believing that the LBW law (which continues "The off side of the striker's wicket shall be determined by the striker's stance at the moment the ball comes into play for that delivery") adequately covers the scenario. They cited the variations bowlers can make, such as bowling a googly or a slower ball, and also the inherent risk in the shot to the batsman, in the justification of their decision.

There are still calls for further review of the stroke, with Jonathan Agnew giving a scenario in which a right-handed batsman can take his stance as a left-hander, then switch stance as the bowler runs in, thus being able to kick away any balls that land outside his now off stump. He also calls for the wide law to be adjusted in one-day cricket, as bowlers are penalised for most deliveries that pass down the leg side.

- **Kevin Pietersen England captaincy**

Pietersen captained England in the fifth ODI against New Zealand after Paul Collingwood was banned for four games for a slow over-rate during the previous match. Pietersen was named as the stand-in captain for three further matches in August.

Pietersen on his first day as England Test captain at The Oval in August 2008 With Michael Vaughan as captain for the first three tests, Pietersen seemed to thrive in his first Test series against his former countrymen scoring 152 in the opening match of the series. During the third Test against South Africa, Pietersen was criticised for throwing his wicket away attempting a six to complete a century when on 94. Jonathan Agnew and Alec Stewart called the stroke "irresponsible" and Agnew continued, suggesting that Pietersen therefore ruled himself out of the potential reckoning for the England captaincy with Vaughan's place in the starting line-up in doubt after failing to score runs. In the event, having lost the match, Vaughan resigned and Pietersen was made the permanent captain of both the Test and ODI sides (Paul Collingwood relinquished the ODI captaincy at the same time).

Following the news that he had been made England Test and ODI captain, Pietersen paid tribute to both outgoing captains but announced that he would look to captain the team in his own style. He scored a century in his debut match as captain in the dead rubber fourth Test, and went on to defeat South Africa 4–0 in the ODI matches. In that series he made 90 not out and got 2–22 with the ball. In the fourth ODI, another dead rubber as England were 3–0 up, he hit a quick 40 to guide England to victory.

In January 2009, following England's losses in India, the media reported that Pietersen had asked the England and Wales Cricket Board (ECB) to hold emergency meetings to discuss Moores' coaching role with the team. Days later, Pietersen made remarks to the media about there being an 'unhealthy situation' that needed to be resolved in the England camp. The media speculated that Moores would shortly be replaced if there was a Pietersen–Moores rift. Moores and Pietersen were believed to be in disagreement on several issues, including the team's training regimen, and the possible selection of former England captain Michael Vaughan for the upcoming tour of the West Indies.

On 7 January 2009, Moores was removed as England's coach by the ECB, and Pietersen unexpectedly resigned as captain. In the immediate aftermath of Pietersen's resignation, several commentators connected with English cricket indicated that they believed that Pietersen had miscalculated by openly advocating for the removal of Moores, particularly in making their dispute public. In an interview several days after his resignation, Pietersen revealed that he had not intended to resign as captain, but was told by ECB officials that he was resigning. Dennis Amiss, the vice-chairman of the ECB, went on record backing up Pietersen in his statement that the story of the rift with Moores had not been leaked to the media by him, saying, "We don't believe Kevin Pietersen leaked the information, we understand his frustration at it being leaked by other parties." Pietersen was captain for three Test matches, and 10 One Day International matches. It was announced that Andrew Strauss would take over the captaincy.

- **Kevin Pietersen Career in 2009**

Pietersen's first match after resigning from the captaincy garnered much media attention, played in the Caribbean during England's tour of the West Indies under the new captain, Strauss. Though Pietersen scored 97 in the first innings of the first Test, West Indies had a lead of 74 and England were bowled out for 51 with Pietersen making only one, being bowled by an out-swinger by Jerome Taylor as England collapsed to an innings defeat. After the second Test was abandoned, Pietersen made 51 in a quickly scheduled 'third' Test. His good form carried on as he scored 72 not out to give England the draw at Barbados. In the fifth and final Test, with England needing to win, Pietersen hit his quickest test century with 102 off 92 balls. He struggled in the one-day series that followed with his top score being 48.

- **Kevin Pietersen in Indian Premier League**

In February 2009, Royal Challengers Bangalore of the Indian Premier League bought Pietersen for US$1,550,000, which made him the highest-paid IPL player along with Andrew Flintoff. The following month RCB owner Vijay Mallya announced that Pietersen would succeed Rahul Dravid as captain. He won two out of his six matches in charge before leaving to fulfil his international commitments with England; Anil Kumble took over the captaincy and led the Bangalore team to the IPL final. Kevin Pietersen was later bought by Deccan Chargers for the 2011 season and was sold to Delhi Daredevils in the 2012 season without having played a single game for the Chargers.

- **West Indies and the ICC World Twenty20**

Pietersen began 2009 with questions over his form, where many pundits viewed him to be in a slump. He was dismissed first ball in the first Test against the touring West Indies side dismissed by the full, swinging ball (a delivery which he seemed to struggle against), but in the second Test made a quick 49 before falling to an attacking shot.

He then suffered what seemed only a minor right Achilles injury and was subsequently ruled out of the ODI series, which England also won. In June 2009, Pietersen played in England's World Twenty20 warm-up match against Scotland, registering an unbeaten 53 in a six-wicket England victory. He also appeared in the news after accidentally hitting a 15-year-old school boy with a cricket ball from a straight-drive after the boy had bowled to him. Pietersen left the boy, from Suffolk, with a signed bat as compensation.

Pietersen's Achilles injury began flared up ahead of England's first Twenty20 match, against the Netherlands not long after. In Pietersen's absence, England incurred a historic loss against the Dutch. He returned for the second match against Pakistan and top scored with 58 off 38 balls and hit 3 sixes (one of which was measured at over 100m) in the 48 run victory, he also top scored in the three run win over India later in the competition. Despite missing the first match Pietersen ended the tournament as England's leading runscorer with 154 at an average of 38.50. He was named in the 'Team of the Tournament' by Cricinfo for the 2009 T20I World Cup.

- **Kevin Pietersen in 2009 Ashes**

Pietersen joined the England Ashes squad in June 2009 for the upcoming 2009 Ashes series. Despite failing to surpass single figure scores during a warm-up match against Warwickshire, he helped England to a score over 400 on 8 July during the first day of the first Test at the SWALEC Stadium, Cardiff with 69 before being dismissed by Nathan Hauritz, top-edging a sweep to a ball outside off stump; the dismissal was heavily criticised. He also seemed to flare up his Achilles injury again suddenly which hampered his batting a bit. In the second innings he was bowled for 8 after leaving a straight ball from Ben Hilfenhaus. Many pundits thought the criticism of England's key batsman from the first innings possibly affected him.

In the first innings at Lords, after proving his fitness, he came at 222–2 and played some trademark shots before being caught behind off Peter Siddle. In the second innings he came in when England had a lead of almost 300 and he and Ravi Bopara batted for time. Pietersen limped when he ran and many shots ran off the inside edge which raised serious doubts for the rest of the series. He actually did well to reach 44 before being caught behind off Siddle again. After struggling in the field as England won, Pietersen was ruled out of the rest of the series with an Achilles injury. This brought to an end 54 consecutive Test matches. As his recovery slowed, Pietersen was not included in the 2009 ICC Champions Trophy and Andy Flower speculated that due to an infection of the wound Pietersen "may miss this winter's tour of South Africa because of slow progress in recovery from surgery."

- **Kevin Pietersen Career in 2010**

Pietersen returned from injury in time to play a part in the 2009–10 winter tour of South Africa. His contributions, nevertheless, were significantly below his pre-injury range with an average of just 27. He showed several lapses of concentration, leading some to suggest that off-field distractions and lingering issues with his removal from the captaincy were still affecting his form.

Pietersen went into the two-match tour of Bangladesh on the back of poor performances on his return from injury and led to speculation Pietersen's England place was under pressure. However, an important first innings of 99 in the first Test and a series clinching score of 74 not out in the second, during a stand of 167 not out with Alastair Cook, saw Pietersen return to much more respectable figures. England won the series 2–0 and Pietersen finished with total runs of 250 and an average for the series of 83.33

Pietersen joined up with his Royal Challengers Bangalore team following the conclusion to England's tour of Bangladesh. Pietersen showed further signs of a return to form in the IPL by scoring 236 runs with a high score of 66*, with an average of 59.00, which was the highest in the IPL.

- **Kevin Pietersen in 2010 ICC World Twenty20**

Pietersen was selected in England's 15-man squad for the 2010 ICC World Twenty20 in the West Indies. Pietersen's tournament got off to a poor start as he made was dismissed for duck by Rory Kleinveldt in a warm up match. In England's first match against the West Indies, Pietersen started confidently scoring 24 from 20 balls before being dismissed on the pull by Darren Sammy. Against Ireland, he struggled to get going, scoring a slow 9 from 18 balls. In England's super eights match against Pakistan he scored 73* from 52 balls, guiding England to a 6 wicket win. In the following super eights match against South Africa, Pietersen scored an aggressive 53 runs from 33 balls, contributing to a 94 run partnership with Craig Kieswetter and a 39 run victory for England. For his performance, he was named man of the match.

Following the conclusion of this match, Pietersen returned home to England to be present at the birth of his son. Pietersen returned in time for England's semi-final against Sri Lanka, where he scored a vital 42* from 26 balls, guiding England home to a 7 wicket victory and a place in their first ICC tournament final since the 2004 ICC Champions Trophy. In the final against old foes Australia, he scored 47 runs from 31 balls, which included 4 fours and 1 six. Pietersen shared in a vital stand of 111 with Kieswetter, before holing out to David Warner off the bowling of Steve Smith. Pietersen's knock was vital in helping England secure a 7 wicket victory and their first ever major ICC tournament victory. After the match Pietersen was named man of the series for his vital contributions with the bat, which ended with Pietersen being the second highest run scorer with 248 runs at an average of 62.00 and a strike rate of 137.77.

- **Bangladesh, Australia and Pakistan**

Pietersen walks out to bat against Australia at the Rose Bowl in his 100th ODI.Pietersen played in the Bangladesh home series, however contributed only 18 in the first innings before assisting England in chasing down a modest total with 10*. He made 64 in the second Test, however. After the Test series, attention was drawn to Pietersen's lack of games for Hampshire – having not played a County Championship at the Rose Bowl since 2005. Having made one Twenty20 appearance for them against Surrey after the Bangladesh Test series, it was announced that he would be leaving Hampshire, stating that "Geographically it just doesn't work. I live in Chelsea." On 22 June, Pietersen played his 100th ODI against Australia at his home ground, the Rose

Bowl.

- **Pietersen bowled for 9 in the first Test v Pakistan at Trent Bridge July 2010**

Pietersen struggled for form in an ODI series against Australia and then a Test series against Pakistan. England beat Australia 3–2, but Pietersen could only manage a top-score of 33. England beat Pakistan 3–1, and although Pietersen top-scored for England with 80 in the second Test, it was the only time he passed 50 and ended the series with a golden duck. His poor form, and an admission by Pietersen before the final Test that he was low on confidence, led to many in the media, including Geoffrey Boycott, to suggest that Pietersen could do with playing County Cricket to regain his form before the 2010–11 Ashes series.

Pietersen was omitted from both of England's limited-overs squads to face Pakistan. However, the ECB brokered a loan move to Surrey for the remainder of the 2010 English cricket season which enables him to play first-class cricket whilst the England side plays Pakistan in the limited overs leg of the tour. Pietersen announced the omission and loan-move to Surrey early through a Twitter message, which contained a swear-word and was quickly removed, and he apologised the following day. The online outburst drew some criticism of him, with national selector Geoff Miller one of those criticising the message. During the lead up to the 2010/11 Ashes Series Pietersen signed up for two first-class games in the South African competition with the KwaZulu Natal Dolphins.

Pietersen went into the 2010–11 Ashes series without a century since March 2009, and many felt that England would be unable to retain the Ashes unless he found form. In the first Test at the Gabba, Brisbane, Pietersen hit 43 in the first innings but wasn't required in the second as England posted 517–1 declared before a draw was declared.

In the second Test in Adelaide, where he hit 158 on the previous Ashes tour, Pietersen joined opener Alastair Cook (148) to make a century partnership before going on to score his 17th Test century. He finished with 227, a Test-best and his second Test double-century, as England declared on 620–5. Given a rare bowl at the end of the fourth day, Pietersen claimed the wicket of Michael Clarke (80) to leave Australia 238–4. England then proceeded to bowl Australia out in the final morning to win by an innings and 71 runs, and Pietersen was named man-of-the-match.

- **Kevin Pietersen in 2011 ODI series against Australia**

In the ODI series that followed the Ashes Test Series Pietersen's performance was solid in the first ODI at the MCG. His team high score of 78 helping England to post a traditionally competitive near 300 score. England were however defeated by the chasing Australians after Shane Watson's monumental 161 not out. After making a first ball duck in the second ODI at Hobart Pietersen's fitness once again became an issue and he missed the third ODI due to a "groin strain". The fourth ODI, despite Pietersen making only 12 with the bat, was won by England. On 29 January Kevin announced to the media that England could make a miraculous comeback to win the series from 3–1 down. In the three remaining matches (all England defeats) Pietersen scored 40, 29 and 26 respectively. Australia won the seven match ODI series 6–1.

- **Kevin Pietersen in Career in 2011**

Pietersen batting during his innings of 72 against Sri Lanka at Lord's.Pietersen was part of England's 15-man squad for the 2011 World Cup hosted by Bangladesh, India and Sri Lanka between February and March. In the warm-up matches he was asked to open the batting in anticipation that he would assume the position for the whole tournament. He had opened the batting just six times in one-day games and never for England, although had done so for England A in 2004. Pietersen returned home early due to injury. A hernia required immediate surgery and the recovery time of around six weeks meant he would miss the rest of the tournament and potentially the IPL. Eoin Morgan took Pietersen's place in the squad. Pietersen earned some criticism after being sighted at a nightclub in London while injured, however he dismissed the criticism as unwarranted.

He returned from injury for the home series against Sri Lanka in May 2011.Pietersen was also picked to play against India in July 2011, and scored 202 not out at Lord's in the 1st Test. During the innings, Pietersen passed 6,000 runs in Tests. The feat took exactly six years, which is the fastest in terms of time taken, and 128 innings. In the fourth Test he scored 175 runs and shared a partnership of 350 runs with Ian Bell. Pietersen was rested for the ODI series against that followed the Tests.

- **Kevin Pietersen in Career in 2012**

Pietersen played a pivotal role in England's tour of Sri Lanka. By scoring a century in the second of two Tests, not only did he move to 20 centuries for England, but he levelled the series at 1–1, ensuring England retain their No.1 Test Ranking status. On 10 April, Pietersen started his first match in the 2012 Indian Premier League for his new team, the Delhi Daredevils. He scored his maiden century in that format during the tournament.

In May 2012, Pietersen was fined for a Twitter outburst against ex-England opener, Nick Knight. He commented "Can somebody please tell me how Knight has worked his way into the commentary box for Tests? Ridiculous" and despite attempts by Cook to "downplay" the incident, the ECB elected to uphold the fine. It was Pietersen's second controversial use of the social media system following the incident in September 2010 where he announced his own dropping from the one-day team, for which he was also fined.

- **Kevin Pietersen Retirement from ODI and T20**

Pietersen batting for Surrey against Somerset after his ODI retirement.On 31 May 2012, Pietersen announced his retirement from one-day international cricket. Although he intended to still play Twenty20s for England, and especially the World Twenty20 tournament in September 2012, the terms of his central contract meant that he had to retire from both forms. Remaining available for Test cricket only, Pietersen said that "with the intensity of the international schedule and the increasing demands on my body, I think it is the right time to step aside and let the next generation of players come through to gain experience for the World Cup in 2015."This announcement came on the back of his 80 against the West Indies at Trent Bridge as England took an unassailable 2–0 lead in the three-Test series. However, on 9 July 2012, Pietersen reversed his decision and suggested that he may return to ODIs in the future.

- **Kevin Pietersen South Africa in the summer of 2012**

After the second Test against South Africa during the latter's tour of England in the summer of 2012, in which Pietersen scored his 21st Test century (149) and took Test-best bowling figures (3–52), Pietersen suggested that the third and final Test of that series might be his last. In the same press conference, he also mentioned issues within the dressing room that needed to be resolved. In the following days, allegations were made that he sent defamatory text messages to members of the South African dressing room, with Strauss and Flower said to be referred to within the messages.

Following talks with the ECB, however, Pietersen then unreservedly committed his future to all forms of cricket for England in a video interview posted on YouTube. He was dropped for the third Test after failing to provide clarification about those messages, despite announcement of the squad being delayed to provide more time for him to do so. He was replaced by Jonny Bairstow.

- **Reintegration and comeback**

In October 2012, ECB confirmed that they had a process which could lead to Pietersen's return to the English cricket team. This led to Pietersen's selection as part of the Test squad later that month. He toured India with a successful England team under Cook, scoring 338 runs in four Tests including a century and two fifties. The century, in the second of four Tests, took Pietersen to 22 Test hundreds, level with the England record. That century was named as third best Test innings of the decade by Wisden in 2019. Cook, however, proceeded to break the record by scoring his twenty-third hundred during the same series. Pietersen also featured in the tour's ODI series, scoring 185 runs across a five-match series that ended in an English defeat.

- **Kevin Pietersen batting during the 2013 Ashes**

Pietersen featured in the three-Test series in New Zealand in February 2013, scoring 73 in the second match. A knee injury forced him to miss the return home series in May that year, however, and prompted fears over fitness for the upcoming 2013 Ashes series. Though he did not play against New Zealand, the ECB remained hopeful over his ability to play against Australia come the summer. On 3 August 2013, Pietersen not only scored a century in the third Ashes series match in the first innings, he became the highest run scorer for England across all forms of cricket combined.

- **Kevin Pietersen in 2014**

His return Ashes tour over the winter of 2013–14 was less successful, however. In a series which England lost 5–0, Pietersen averaged only 29 and passed fifty only twice in ten innings. He made his 100th Test appearance in the first Test. During this game Pietersen was dismissed by a widely reported catch taken by Chris Sabburg, who entered the field as a substitute fielder. He remained nevertheless England's leading run scorer with 294 runs.

He also bowled during the fifth and final Test. Once the tour had ended, and the fallout had contributed to the removal of Flower as head coach, there was much media speculation on the nature of Pietersen's relationship with the team management. The ECB met and announced on 4 February 2014 that Pietersen had not been selected for the upcoming tour of the Caribbean, a decision they described as "unanimous". Media announcements immediately began stating that Pietersen's career was over. Pietersen himself released a statement which read "Although I am obviously very sad the incredible journey has come to an end, I'm also hugely proud of what we, as a team, have achieved over the past nine years."

- **Kevin Pietersen Awards**

Pietersen gained several awards for his performances in the 2005 season. He was named both the ICC 'ODI Player of the Year' and 'Emerging Player of the Year' in 2005, and was one of the five Wisden Cricketers of the Year (alongside team mates Simon Jones and Matthew Hoggard) for his role in the successful 2005 Ashes series against Australia. Along with the rest of the England team, Pietersen was recognised in the 2006 New Year Honours, being appointed a Member of the Order of the British Empire for services to cricket. He also played for the ICC World XI in the 2005 ICC Super Series against Australia.

- **Kevin Pietersen Records**

1. Second-highest run-total from his first 25 Tests (behind Sir Don Bradman).
2. Fourth Englishman to make the top score in both innings of debut Test.
3. One of only twenty-five players to have a peak ICC batting rating over 900.

4. Achieved 5,000 Test runs in the fastest time, reaching this feat in 4 years and 243 days.

TWO

ENGLAND CRICKET TEAM

- **England cricket team**

The England cricket team represents England and Wales in international cricket. Since 1997, it has been governed by the England and Wales Cricket Board (ECB), having been previously governed by Marylebone Cricket Club (the MCC) since 1903. England, as a founding nation, is a Full Member of the International Cricket Council (ICC) with Test, One Day International (ODI) and Twenty20 International (T20I) status. Until the 1990s, Scottish and Irish players also played for England as those countries were not yet ICC members in their own right.

England and Australia were the first teams to play a Test match (15–19 March 1877), and along with South Africa, these nations formed the Imperial Cricket Conference (the predecessor to today's International Cricket Council) on 15 June 1909. England and Australia also played the first ODI on 5 January 1971. England's first T20I was played on 13 June

2005, once more against Australia.

As of 20 December 2022, England have played 1,058 Test matches, winning 387 and losing 317 (with 354 draws). In Test series against Australia, England play for The Ashes, one of the most famous trophies in all of sport, and they have won the urn on 32 occasions. England have also played 773 ODIs, winning 389. They have appeared in the final of the Cricket World Cup four times, winning once in 2019; they have also finished as runners-up in two ICC Champions Trophies (2004 and 2013). England have played 170 T20Is, winning 90. They won the ICC T20 World Cup in 2010 and 2022, and were runners-up in 2016.As of 20 December 2022, England are ranked third in Tests, second in ODIs and second in T20Is by the ICC.

- **The All-England Eleven in 1846**

The first recorded incidence of a team with a claim to represent England comes from 9 July 1739 when an "All-England" team, which consisted of 11 gentlemen from any part of England exclusive of Kent, played against "the Unconquerable County" of Kent and lost by a margin of "very few notches". Such matches were repeated on numerous occasions for the best part of a century.In 1846 William Clarke formed the All-England Eleven. This team eventually competed against a United All-England Eleven with annual matches occurring between 1847 and 1856. These matches were arguably the most important contest of the English season if judged by the quality of the players.

- **The 1859 English team to North America.**

The first overseas tour occurred in September 1859 with England touring North America. This team had six players from the All-England Eleven, six from the United All-England Eleven and was captained by George Parr.With the outbreak of the American Civil War, attention turned elsewhere. English tourists visited Australia in 1861–62 with this first tour organised as a commercial venture by Messrs Spiers and Pond, restaurateurs of Melbourne. Most matches played during tours prior to 1877 were "against odds", with the opposing team fielding more than 11 players to make for a more even contest. This first Australian tour were mostly against odds of at least 18/11.

- **The first England team to tour southern Australia in 1861–62**

The tour was so successful that Parr led a second tour in 1863–64. James Lillywhite led a subsequent England team which sailed on the P&O steamship Poonah on 21 September 1876. They played a combined Australian XI, for once on even terms of 11-a-side. The match, starting on 15 March 1877 at the Melbourne Cricket Ground came to be regarded as the inaugural Test match. The combined Australian XI won this Test match by 45 runs with Charles Bannerman of Australia scoring the first Test century. At the time, the match was promoted as James Lillywhite's XI v Combined Victoria and New South Wales. The teams played a return match on the same ground at Easter, 1877, when Lillywhite's team avenged their loss with a victory by four wickets. The first Test match on English soil occurred in 1880 with England victorious; this was the first time England fielded a fully representative side with W. G. Grace included in the team.

- **1880s**

As a result of this loss, the tour of 1882–83 was dubbed by England captain Ivo Bligh as "the quest to regain the ashes". England, with a mixture of amateurs and professionals, won the series 2–1. Bligh was presented with an urn that contained some ashes, which have variously been said to be of a bail, ball or even a woman's veil, and so The Ashes was born. A fourth match was then played which Australia won by four wickets. However, the match was not considered part of the Ashes series. England dominated many of these early contests, with England winning the Ashes series 10 times between 1884 and 1898. During this period England also played their first Test match against South Africa in 1889 at Port Elizabeth.

- **1890s**

England won the 1890 Ashes series 2–0, with the third match of the series being the first Test match to be abandoned. England lost 2–1 in the 1891–92 series, although England regained the urn the following year. England again won the 1894–95 series, winning 3–2 under the leadership of Andrew Stoddart. In 1895–96, England played South Africa, winning all Tests in the series. The 1899 Ashes series was the first tour where the MCC and the counties appointed a selection committee. There were three active players: Grace, Lord Hawke and Warwickshire captain Herbert Bainbridge. Prior to this, England teams for home Tests had been chosen by the club on whose ground the match was to be played. England lost the 1899 Ashes series 1–0, with Grace making his final Test appearance in the first match of the series.

- **1900s**

The start of the 20th century saw mixed results for England as they lost four of the eight Ashes series between 1900 and 1914. During this period, England lost their first series against South Africa in the 1905–06 season 4–1 as their batting faltered.England lost their first series of the new century to Australia in 1901–02 Ashes. Australia also won the 1902 series, which was memorable for exciting cricket, including Gilbert Jessop scoring a Test century in just 70 minutes. England regained the Ashes in 1904 under the captaincy of Pelham Warner. R. E. Foster scored 287 on his debut and Wilfred Rhodes took 15 wickets in a match. In 1905–06, England lost 4–1 against South Africa. England avenged the defeat in 1907, when they won the series 1–0 under the captaincy of Foster. However, they lost the 1909 Ashes series against Australia, suing 25 players in the process. England also lost to South Africa, with Jack Hobbs scoring his first of 15 centuries on the tour.

- **1910s**

England toured Australia in 1911–12 and beat their opponents 4–1. The team included the likes of Rhodes, Hobbs, Frank Woolley and Sydney Barnes. England lost the first match of the series but bounced back and won the next four Tests. This proved to be the last Ashes series before the war.The 1912 season saw England take part in a unique experiment. A nine-Test triangular tournament involving England, South Africa and Australia was set up. The series was hampered by a very wet summer and player disputes however and the tournament was considered a failure with the Daily Telegraph stating.Nine Tests provide a surfeit of cricket, and contests between Australia and South Africa are not a great attraction to the British public.

With Australia sending a weakened team and the South African bowlers being ineffective England dominated the tournament winning four of their six matches. The match between Australia and South Africa at Lord's was visited by King George V, the first time a reigning monarch had watched Test cricket. England went on one more tour before the outbreak of the First World War, beating South Africa 4–0, with Barnes taking 49 wickets in the series.

- **1920s**

English cricket team at the Test match at the Brisbane Exhibition Ground in 1928. England won by a record margin of 675 runs.England's first match after the war was in the 1920–21 season against Australia. Still feeling the effects of the war England went down to a series of crushing defeats and suffered their first whitewash losing the series 5–0. Six Australians scored hundreds while Mailey spun out 36 English batsmen. Things were no better in the next few Ashes series losing the 1921 Ashes series 3–0 and the 1924–25 Ashes 4–1. England's fortunes were to change in 1926 as they regained the Ashes and were a formidable team during this period dispatching Australia 4–1 in the 1928–29 Ashes tour.

On the same year the West Indies became the fourth nation to be granted Test status and played their first game against England. England won each of these three Tests by an innings, and a view was expressed in the press that their elevation had proved a mistake although Learie Constantine did the double on the tour. In the 1929–30 season England went on two concurrent tours with one team going to New Zealand (who were granted Test status earlier that year) and the other to the West Indies. Despite sending two separate teams England won both tours beating New Zealand 1–0 and the West Indies 2–1.

- **1930s**

Bill Woodfull evades a Bodyline ball. Note the number of leg-side fielders.The 1930 Ashes series saw a young Don Bradman dominate the tour, scoring 974 runs in his seven Test innings. He scored 254 at Lord's, 334 at Headingley and 232 at The Oval. Australia regained the Ashes winning the series 3–1. As a result of Bradman's prolific run-scoring the England captain Douglas Jardine chose to develop the already existing leg theory into fast leg theory, or bodyline, as a tactic to stop Bradman. Fast leg theory involved bowling fast balls directly at the batsman's body. The batsman would need to defend himself, and if he touched the ball with the bat, he risked being caught by one of a large number of fielders placed on the leg side.

Using Jardine's fast leg theory, England won the next Ashes series 4–1, but complaints about the Bodyline tactic caused crowd disruption on the tour, and threats of diplomatic action from the Australian Cricket Board, which during the tour sent the following cable to the MCC in London:

Bodyline bowling assumed such proportions as to menace best interests of game, making protection of body by batsmen the main consideration. Causing intensely bitter feeling between players as well as injury. In our opinion is unsportsmanlike. Unless stopped at once likely to upset friendly relations existing between Australia and England.Later, Jardine was removed from the captaincy and the Laws of Cricket changed so that no more than one fast ball aimed at the body was permitted per over, and having more than two fielders behind square leg was banned.

England's following tour of India in the 1933–34 season was the first Test match to be staged in the subcontinent. The series was also notable for Stan Nichols and Nobby Clark bowling so many bouncers that the Indian batsman wore solar toupées instead of caps to protect themselves.Australia won the 1934 Ashes series 2–1 and kept the urn for the following 19 years. Many of the wickets of the time were friendly to batsmen resulting in a large proportion of matches ending in high scoring draws and many batting records being set.

England drew the 1938 Ashes, meaning Australia retained the urn. England went into the final match of the series at The Oval 1–0 down, but won the final game by an innings and 579 runs. Len Hutton made the highest ever Test score by an Englishman, making 364 in England first innings to help them reach 903, their highest ever score against Australia.

The 1938–39 tour of South Africa saw another experiment with the deciding Test being a timeless Test that was played to a finish. England lead 1–0 going into the final timeless match at Durban. Despite the final Test being 'timeless', the game ended in a draw after 10 days as England had to catch the train to catch the boat home. A record 1,981 runs were scored, and the concept of timeless Tests was abandoned. England went on one final tour of the West Indies in 1939 before the Second World War, although a team for an MCC tour of India was selected more in hope than expectation of the matches being played.

- **1940s**

Test cricket resumed after the war in 1946, and England won their first match back against India. However, they struggled in the 1946–47 Ashes series, losing 3–0 in Australia under Wally Hammond's captaincy. England beat South Africa 3–0 in 1947 with Denis Compton scoring 1,187 runs in the series.

The 1947–48 series against the West Indies was another disappointment for England, with the side losing 2–0 following injuries to several key players. England suffered further humiliation against Bradman's invincible side in the 1948 Ashes series. Hutton was controversially dropped for the third Test, and England were bowled out for just 52 at The Oval. The series proved to be Bradman's final Ashes series.

In 1948–49, England beat South Africa 2–0 under the captaincy of George Mann. The series included a record breaking stand of 359 between Hutton and Cyril Washbrook. The decade ended with England drawing the Test series against New Zealand, with every match ending in a draw.

- **1950s**

Their fortunes changed on the 1953 Ashes tour as they won the series 1–0. England did not lose a series between their 1950–51 and 1958–59 tours of Australia and secured famous victory in 1954–55 under the captaincy of Len Hutton, thanks to Frank Tyson whose 6/85 at Sydney and 7/27 at Melbourne are remembered as the fastest bowling ever seen in Australia. The 1956 series was remembered for the bowling of Jim Laker who took 46 wickets at an average of 9.62, including figures of 19/90 at Old Trafford. After drawing to South Africa, England defeated the West Indies and New Zealand comfortably.

The England team then left for Australia in the 1958–59 season with a team that had been hailed as the strongest ever to leave on an Ashes tour but lost the series 4–0 as Richie Benaud's revitalised Australians were too strong, with England struggling with the bat throughout the series.On 24 August 1959, England inflicted its only 5–0 whitewash over India. All out for 194 at The Oval, India lost the last test by an innings. England's batsman Ken Barrington and Colin Cowdrey both had an excellent series with the bat, with Barrington scoring 357 runs across the series and Cowdrey scoring 344.

- **1960s**

The early and middle 1960s were poor periods for English cricket. Despite England's strength on paper, Australia held the Ashes and the West Indies dominated England in the early part of the decade. May stood down as captain in 1961 following the 1961 Ashes defeat.

Ted Dexter succeeded him as captain but England continued to suffer indifferent results. In 1961–62, they beat Pakistan, but also lost to India. The following year saw England and Australia tie the 1962–63 Ashes series 1–1, meaning Australia retained the urn. Despite beating New Zealand 3–0, England went on to lose to the West Indies, and again failed in the 1964 Ashes, losing the home series 1–0, which marked the end of Dexter's captaincy.

However, from 1968 to 1971 they played 27 consecutive Test matches without defeat, winning 9 and drawing 18 (including the abandoned Test at Melbourne in 1970–71). The sequence began when they drew with Australia at Lord's in the Second Test of the 1968 Ashes series and ended in 1971 when India won the Third Test at The Oval by four wickets. They played 13 Tests with only one defeat immediately beforehand and so played a total of 40 consecutive Tests with only one defeat, dating from their innings victory over the West Indies at The Oval in 1966. During this period they beat New Zealand, India, the West Indies, and Pakistan, and under Ray Illingworth's leadership, regained The Ashes from Australia in 1970–71.

- **1970s**

The 1970s, for the England team, can be largely split into three parts. Early in the decade, Illingworth's side dominated world cricket, winning the Ashes away in 1971 and then retaining them at home in 1972. The same side beat Pakistan at home in 1971 and played by far the better cricket against India that season. However, England were largely helped by the rain to sneak the Pakistan series 1–0 but the same rain saved India twice and one England collapse saw them lose to India. This was, however, one of (if not the) strongest England team ever with the likes of Illingworth, Geoffrey Boycott, John Edrich, Basil D'Oliveira, Dennis Amiss, Alan Knott, John Snow and Derek Underwood at its core.

The mid-1970s were more turbulent. Illingworth and several others had refused to tour India in 1972–73 which led to a clamour for Illingworth's job by the end of that summer – England had just been beaten 2–0 by a flamboyant West Indies side – with several England players well over 35. Mike Denness was the surprising choice but only lasted 18 months; his results against poor opposition were good, but England were badly exposed as ageing and lacking in good fast bowling against the 1974–75

Australians, losing that series 4–1 to lose the Ashes.Denness was replaced in 1975 by Tony Greig. While he managed to avoid losing to Australia, his side were largely thrashed the following year by the young and very much upcoming West Indies for whom Greig's infamous "grovel" remark acted as motivation. Greig's finest hour was probably the 1976–77 win over India in India. When Greig was discovered as being instrumental in World Series Cricket, he was sacked, and replaced by Mike Brearley.

Brearley's side showed again the hyperbole that is often spoken when one side dominates in cricket. While his side of 1977–80 contained some young players who went on to become England greats, most notably future captains Ian Botham, David Gower and Graham Gooch, their opponents were often very much weakened by the absence of their World Series players, especially in 1978, when England beat New Zealand 3–0 and Pakistan 2–0 before thrashing what was effectively Australia's 2nd XI 5–1 in 1978–79.

- **1980s**

The England team, with Brearley's exit in 1980, was never truly settled throughout the 1980s, which will probably be remembered as a low point for the team. While some of the great players like Botham, Gooch and Gower had fine careers, the team seldom succeeded in beating good opposition throughout the decade and did not score a home Test victory (except against minnows Sri Lanka) between September 1985 and July 1990.

Botham took over the captaincy in 1980 and they put up a good fight against the West Indies, losing a five match Test series 1–0, although England were humbled in the return series. After scoring a pair in the first Test against Australia,

Botham lost the captaincy due to his poor form, and was replaced by Brearley. Botham returned to form and played exceptionally in the remainder of the series, being named man of the match in the third, fourth and fifth Tests. The series became known as Botham's Ashes as England recorded a 3–1 victory.

Keith Fletcher took over as captain in 1981, but England lost his first series in charge against India. Bob Willis took over as captain in 1982 and enjoyed victories over India and Pakistan, but lost the Ashes after Australia clinched the series 2–1. England hosted the World Cup in 1983 and reached the semi-finals, but their Test form remained poor, as they suffered defeats against New Zealand, Pakistan and the West Indies.Gower took over as skipper in 1984 and led the team to a 2–1 victory over India. They went on to win the 1985 Ashes 3–1, although after this came a poor run of form. Defeat to the West Indies dented the team's confidence, and they went on to lose to India 2–0. In 1986, Micky Stewart was appointed the first full-time England coach. England beat New Zealand, but there was little hope of them retaining the Ashes in 1986–87. However, despite being described as a team that 'can't bat, can't bowl and can't field', they went on to win the series 2–1.

After losing consecutive series against Pakistan, England drew a three match Test series against New Zealand 0–0. They reached the final of the 1987 World Cup, but lost by seven runs against Australia. After losing 4–0 to the West Indies, England lost the Ashes to a resurgent Australia led by Allan Border. With the likes of Gooch banned following a rebel tour to South Africa, a new look England side suffered defeat again against the West Indies, although this time by a margin of 2–1.

- **1990s**

If the 1980s were a low point for English Test cricket, then the 1990s were only a slight improvement. The arrival of Gooch as captain in 1990 forced a move toward more professionalism and especially fitness though it took some time for old habits to die. Even in 2011, one or two successful county players have been shown up as physically unfit for international cricket. Creditable performances against India and New Zealand in 1990 were followed by a hard-fought draw against the 1991 West Indies and a strong performance in the 1992 Cricket World Cup in which the England team finished as runners-up for the second consecutive World Cup, but landmark losses against Australia in 1990–91 and especially Pakistan in 1992 showed England up badly in terms of bowling. So bad was England's bowling in 1993 that Rod Marsh described England's pace attack at one point as "pie throwers". Having lost three of the first four Tests played in England in 1993, Gooch resigned to be replaced by Michael Atherton.

More selectorial problems abounded during Atherton's reign as new chairman of selectors and coach Ray Illingworth (then into his 60s) assumed almost sole responsibility for the team off the field. The youth policy which had seen England emerge from the West Indies tour of 1993–94 with some credit (though losing to a seasoned Windies team) was abandoned and players such as Gatting and Gooch were persisted with when well into their 30s and 40s. England continued to do well at home against weaker opponents such as India, New Zealand and a West Indies side beginning to fade but struggled badly against improving sides like Pakistan and South Africa. Atherton had offered his resignation after losing the 1997 Ashes series 3–2 having been 1–0 up after two matches – eventually to resign one series later in early 1998. England, looking for talent, went through a whole raft of new players during this period, such as Ronnie Irani, Adam Hollioake, Craig White, Graeme Hick and Mark Ramprakash. At this time, there were two main problems:

The lack of a genuine all-rounder to bat at 6, Botham having left a huge gap in the batting order when he retired from Tests in 1992.Alec Stewart, a sound wicket-keeper and an excellent player of quick bowling, could not open and keep wicket, hence his batting down the order, where he was often exposed to spin which he did not play as well.

Stewart took the reins as captain in 1998, but another losing Ashes series and early World Cup exit cost him Test and ODI captaincy in 1999. This should not detract from the 1998 home Test series where England showed great fortitude to beat a powerful South African side 2–1.

Another reason for their poor performances were the demands of County Cricket teams on their players, meaning that England could rarely field a full-strength team on their tours. This eventually led to the ECB taking over from the MCC as the governing body of England and the implementation of central contracts. 1992 also saw Scotland sever ties with the England and Wales team, and begin to compete as the Scotland national team.

By 1999, with coach David Lloyd resigning after the World Cup exit and new captain Nasser Hussain just appointed, England hit rock bottom (literally ranked as the lowest-rated Test nation) after losing 2–1 to New Zealand in shambolic fashion. Hussain was booed on the Oval balcony as the crowd jeered "We've got the worst team in the world" to the tune of "He's Got the Whole World in His Hands".

- **2000s**

Central contracts were installed – reducing players workloads – and following the arrival of Zimbabwean coach Duncan Fletcher, England thrashed the fallen West Indies 3–1. England's results in Asia improved that winter with series wins against both Pakistan and Sri Lanka. Hussain's side had a far harder edge to it, avoiding the anticipated "Greenwash" in the 2001 Ashes series against the all-powerful Australian team. The nucleus the side was slowly coming together as players such as Hussain himself, Graham Thorpe, Darren Gough and Ashley Giles began to be regularly selected. By 2003 though, having endured another Ashes drubbing as well as another first-round exit from the World Cup, Hussain resigned as captain after one Test against South Africa.

Michael Vaughan took over, with players encouraged to express themselves. England won five consecutive Test series prior to facing Australia in the 2005 Ashes series, taking the team to second place in the ICC Test Championship table. During this period England defeated the West Indies home and away, New Zealand, and Bangladesh at home, and South Africa in South Africa. In June 2005, England played its first ever T20 international match, defeating Australia by 100 runs. Later that year, England defeated Australia 2–1 in a thrilling series to regain the Ashes for the first time in 16 years, having lost them in 1989. Following the 2005 Ashes win, the team suffered from a spate of serious injuries to key players such as Vaughan, Giles, Andrew Flintoff and Simon Jones. As a result, the team underwent an enforced period of transition. A 2–0 defeat in Pakistan was followed by two drawn away series with India and Sri Lanka.

In the home Test series victory against Pakistan in July and August 2006, several promising new players emerged. Most notable were the left-arm orthodox spin bowler Monty Panesar, the first Sikh to play Test cricket for England, and left-handed opening batsman Alastair Cook. The 2006–07 Ashes series was keenly anticipated and was expected to provide a level of competition comparable to the 2005 series. In the event, England, captained by Flintoff who was deputising for the injured Vaughan, lost all five Tests to concede the first Ashes whitewash in 86 years.

In the 2007 Cricket World Cup, England lost to most of the Test playing nations they faced, beating only the West Indies and Bangladesh, although they also avoided defeat by any of the non-Test playing nations. Even so, the unimpressive nature of most of their victories in the tournament, combined with heavy defeats by New Zealand, Australia and South Africa, left many commentators criticising the manner in which the England team approached the one-day game. Coach Duncan Fletcher resigned after eight years in the job as a result and was succeeded by former Sussex coach Peter Moores.

In 2007–08, England toured Sri Lanka and New Zealand, losing the first series 1–0 and winning the second 2–1. These series were followed up at home in May 2008 with a 2–0 home series win against New Zealand, with the results easing pressure on Moores – who was not at ease with his team, particularly star batsman Kevin Pietersen. Pietersen succeeded Vaughan as captain in June 2008, after England had been well beaten by South Africa at home. The poor relationship between the two came to a head on the 2008–09 tour to India. England lost the series 1–0 and both men resigned their positions, although Pietersen remained a member of the England team. Moores was replaced as coach by Zimbabwean Andy Flower. Against this background, England toured the West Indies under the captaincy of Andrew Strauss and, in a disappointing performance, lost the Test series 1–0.

The 2009 Ashes series featured the first Test match played in Wales, at Sophia Gardens, Cardiff. England drew the match thanks to a last-wicket stand by bowlers James Anderson and Panesar. A victory for each team followed before the series was decided at The Oval. Thanks to fine bowling by Stuart Broad and Graeme Swann and a debut century by Jonathan Trott, England regained the Ashes.

- **2010s**

2019 World cup winning team with prime minister Theresa May After a drawn Test series in South Africa, England won their first ever ICC world championship, the 2010 World Twenty20, with a seven-wicket win over Australia in Barbados. The following winter in the 2010–11 Ashes, they beat Australia 3–1 to retain the urn and record their first series win in Australia for 24 years. Furthermore, all three of their wins were by an innings – the first time a touring side had ever recorded three innings victories in a single Test series. Cook earned Man of the Series with 766 runs.

England struggled to match their Test form in the 2011 Cricket World Cup. Despite beating South Africa and tying with eventual winners India, England suffered shock losses to Ireland and Bangladesh before losing in the quarter-finals to Sri Lanka. However the team's excellent form in the Test match arena continued and on 13 August 2011, they became the world's top-ranked Test team after comfortably whitewashing India 4–0, their sixth consecutive series victory and eighth in the past nine series. However, this status only lasted a year – having lost 3–0 to Pakistan over the winter, England were beaten 2–0 by South Africa, who replaced them at the top of the rankings. It was their first home series loss since 2008, against the same opposition.

This loss saw the resignation of Strauss as captain (and his retirement from cricket). Cook, who was already in charge of the ODI side, replaced Strauss and led England to a 2–1 victory in India – their first in the country since 1984–85. In doing so, he became the first captain to score centuries in his first five Tests as captain and became England's leading century-maker with 23 centuries to his name.

- **The England team celebrate victory over Australia in the 2015 Ashes series**

After finishing as runners-up in the ICC Champions Trophy, England faced Australia in back-to-back Ashes series. A 3–0 home win secured England the urn for the fourth time in five series. However, in the return series, they found themselves utterly demolished in a 5–0 defeat, their second Ashes whitewash in under a decade. Their misery was compounded by batsman Jonathan Trott leaving the tour early due to a stress-related illness and the mid-series retirement of spinner Graeme Swann. Following the tour, head coach Flower resigned his post while Pietersen was dropped indefinitely from the England team. Flower was replaced by his predecessor, Moores, but he was sacked for a second time after a string of disappointing results including failing to advance from the group stage at the 2015 World Cup. He was replaced by Australian Trevor Bayliss who oversaw an upturn of form in the ODI side, including series victories against New Zealand and Pakistan. In the Test arena, England reclaimed the Ashes 3–2 in the summer of 2015.

England entered the 2019 Cricket World Cup as favourites, having been ranked the number one ODI side by the ICC for over a year prior to the tournament. However, shock defeats to Pakistan and Sri Lanka during the group stage left them on the brink of elimination and needing to win their final two games against India and New Zealand to guarantee progression to the semi-finals. This was achieved, putting their campaign back on track, and an eight-wicket victory over Australia in the semi-final at Edgbaston meant England were in their first World Cup final since 1992. The final against New Zealand at Lord's has been described as one of the greatest and most dramatic matches in the history of cricket, with some calling it the "greatest ODI in history", as both the match and subsequent Super Over were tied, after England went into the final over of their innings 14 runs behind New Zealand's total. England won by virtue of having scored more boundaries throughout the match, securing their maiden World Cup title in their fourth final appearance.

- **England and Wales Cricket Board**

The England and Wales Cricket Board (ECB) is the governing body of English cricket and the England cricket team. The Board has been operating since 1 January 1997 and represents England on the International Cricket Council. The ECB is also responsible for the generation of income from the sale of tickets, sponsorship and broadcasting rights, primarily in relation to the England team. The ECB's income in the 2006 calendar year was £77 million.

Prior to 1997, the Test and County Cricket Board (TCCB) was the governing body for the English team. Apart from in Test matches, when touring abroad, the England team officially played as MCC up to and including the 1976–77 tour of Australia, reflecting the time when MCC had been responsible for selecting the touring party. The last time the England touring team wore the bacon-and-egg colours of the MCC was on the 1996–97 tour of New Zealand.

- **Status of Wales**

Historically, the England team represented the whole of Great Britain in international cricket, with Scottish or Welsh national teams playing sporadically and players from both countries occasionally representing England. Scotland became an independent member of the ICC in 1994, having severed links with the TCCB two years earlier.

Criticism has been made of the England and Wales Cricket Board using only the England name while utilising Welsh players such as Simon and Geraint Jones. With Welsh players pursuing international careers exclusively with an England team, there have been a number of calls for Wales to become an independent member of the ICC, or for the ECB to provide more fixtures for a Welsh national team. However, both Cricket Wales and Glamorgan County Cricket Club have continually supported the ECB, with Glamorgan arguing for the financial benefits of the Welsh county within the English structure, and Cricket Wales stating they are "committed to continuing to play a major role within the ECB"

The absence of a Welsh cricket team has seen a number of debates within the Welsh Senedd. In 2013 a debate saw both Conservative and Labour members lend their support to the establishment of an independent Welsh team.

In 2015, a report produced by the Welsh National Assembly's petitions committee, reflected the passionate debate around the issue. Bethan Jenkins, Plaid Cymru's spokesperson on heritage, culture, sport and broadcasting, and a member of the petitions committee, argued that Wales should have its own international team and withdraw from the ECB. Jenkins noted that Ireland (with a population of 6.4 million) was an ICC member with 6,000 club players whereas Wales (with 3 million) had 7,500. Jenkins said: "Cricket Wales and Glamorgan CCC say the idea of a Welsh national cricket team is 'an emotive subject', of course having a national team is emotive, you only have to look at the stands during any national game to see that. To suggest this as anything other than natural is a bit of a misleading argument."

In 2017, the First Minister of Wales, Carwyn Jones called for the reintroduction of the Welsh one-day team stating: " is odd that we see Ireland and Scotland playing in international tournaments and not Wales."

- **Team colours**

1. 1994–1996Tetley Bitter
2. 1996–1998ASICS
3. 1998–2000Vodafone
4. 2000–2008Admiral
5. 2008–2010Adidas
6. 2010–2014Brit Insurance
7. 2014–2017Waitrose
8. 2017–2021New BalanceNatWest
9. 2021–2022Cinch

10. 2022–presentCastore

In February 2021, England and Wales Cricket Board announced that England's Principal partner NatWest has been replaced by Cinch, an online used car marketplace. England's kit is manufactured by Castore, who replaced previous manufacturer New Balance in April 2022.

When playing Test cricket, England's cricket whites feature the three lions badge on the left of the shirt and the name of the sponsor Cinch on the centre. English fielders may wear a navy blue cap or white sun hat with the ECB logo in the middle. Helmets are also coloured navy blue. Before 1997 the uniform sported the TCCB lion and stumps logo on the uniforms, while the helmets, jumpers and hats had the three lions emblem.

In limited overs cricket, England's ODI and Twenty20 shirts feature the Cinch logo across the centre, with the three lions badge on the left of the shirt and the New Balance logo on the right. In ODIs, the kit comprises a blue shirt with navy trousers, whilst the Twenty20 kit comprises a flame red shirt and navy trousers. In ICC limited-overs tournaments, a modified kit design is used with sponsor's logo moving to the sleeve and 'ENGLAND' printed across the front.Over the years, England's ODI kit has cycled between various shades of blue (such as a pale blue used until the mid-1990s, when it was replaced in favour of a bright blue)with the occasional all-red kit.In April 2017, ECB brought back traditional cable-knit sweater for test matches under new supplier New Balance.

THREE

Let's Know About Cricket

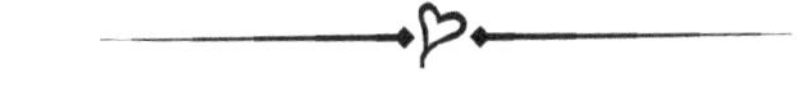

- **Let's Know About Cricket**

Cricket is a bat-and-ball game played between two teams of eleven players on a field at the centre of which is a 22-yard (20-metre) pitch with a wicket at each end, each comprising two bails balanced on three stumps. The game proceeds when a player on the fielding team, called the bowler, "bowls" (propels) the ball from one end of the pitch towards the wicket at the other end. The batting side's players score runs by striking the bowled ball with a bat and running between the wickets, while the bowling side tries to prevent this by keeping the ball within the field and getting it to either wicket, and dismiss each batter (so they are "out"). Means of dismissal include being bowled, when the ball hits the stumps and dislodges the bails, and by the fielding side either catching a hit ball before it touches the ground, or hitting a wicket with the ball before a batter can cross the crease line in front of the wicket to complete a run. When ten batters have been dismissed, the innings ends and the teams swap roles. The game is adjudicated by two umpires, aided by a third umpire and match referee in international matches.

Forms of cricket range from Twenty20, with each team batting for a single innings of 20 overs and the game generally lasting three hours, to Test matches played over five days. Traditionally cricketers play in all-white kit, but in limited overs cricket they wear club or team colours. In addition to the basic kit, some players wear protective gear to prevent injury caused by the ball, which is a hard, solid spheroid made of compressed leather with a slightly raised sewn seam enclosing a cork core layered with tightly wound string.

The earliest reference to cricket is in South East England in the mid-16th century. It spread globally with the expansion of the British Empire, with the first international matches in the second half of the 19th century. The game's governing body is the International Cricket Council (ICC), which has over 100 members, twelve of which are full members who play Test matches. The game's rules, the Laws of Cricket, are maintained by Marylebone Cricket Club (MCC) in London. The sport is followed primarily in South Asia, Australasia, the United Kingdom, southern Africa and the West Indies.Women's cricket, which is organised and played separately, has also achieved international standard. The most successful side playing international cricket is Australia, which has won seven One Day International trophies, including five World Cups, more than any other country and has been the top-rated Test side more than any other country.

- **History of cricket to 1725**

Cricket is one of many games in the "club ball" sphere that basically involve hitting a ball with a hand-held implement; others include baseball (which shares many similarities with cricket, both belonging in the more specific bat-and-ball games category), golf, hockey, tennis, squash, badminton and table tennis. In cricket's case, a key difference is the existence of a solid target structure, the wicket (originally, it is thought, a "wicket gate" through which sheep were herded), that the batter must defend. The cricket historian Harry Altham identified three "groups" of "club ball" games: the "hockey group", in which the ball is driven to and fro between two targets (the goals); the "golf group", in which the ball is driven towards an undefended target (the hole); and the "cricket group", in which "the ball is aimed at a mark (the wicket) and driven away from it".

It is generally believed that cricket originated as a children's game in the south-eastern counties of England, sometime during the medieval period.Although there are claims for prior dates, the earliest definite reference to cricket being played comes from evidence given at a court case in Guildford in January 1597 (Old Style), equating to January 1598 in the modern calendar. The case concerned ownership of a certain plot of land and the court heard the testimony of a 59-year-old coroner, John Derrick, who gave witness that.

Being a scholler in the ffree schoole of Guldeford hee and diverse of his fellows did runne and play there at creckett and other plaies.

Given Derrick's age, it was about half a century earlier when he was at school and so it is certain that cricket was being played c. 1550 by boys in Surrey. The view that it was originally a children's game is reinforced by Randle Cotgrave's 1611 English-French dictionary in which he defined the noun "crosse" as "the crooked staff wherewith boys play at cricket" and the verb form "crosser" as "to play at cricket".

One possible source for the sport's name is the Old English word "cryce" (or "cricc") meaning a crutch or staff. In Samuel Johnson's Dictionary, he derived cricket from "cryce, Saxon, a stick". In Old French, the word "criquet" seems to have meant a kind of club or stick. Given the strong medieval trade connections between south-east England and the County of Flanders when the latter belonged to the Duchy of Burgundy, the name may have been derived from the Middle Dutch (in use in Flanders at the time) "krick"(-e), meaning a stick (crook). Another possible source is the Middle Dutch word "krickstoel", meaning a long low stool used for kneeling in church and which resembled the long low wicket with two stumps used in early cricket. According to Heiner Gillmeister, a European language expert of Bonn University, "cricket" derives from the Middle Dutch phrase for hockey, met de (krik ket)sen (i.e., "with the stick chase"). Gillmeister has suggested that not only the name but also the sport itself may be of Flemish origin.

- **Growth of amateur and professional cricket in England**

Evolution of the cricket bat. The original "hockey stick" (left) evolved into the straight bat from c. 1760 when pitched delivery bowling began.

Although the main object of the game has always been to score the most runs, the early form of cricket differed from the modern game in certain key technical aspects; the North American variant of cricket known as wicket retained many of these aspects. The ball was bowled underarm by the bowler and along the ground towards a batter armed with a bat that in shape resembled a hockey stick; the batter defended a low, two-stump wicket; and runs were called notches because the scorers recorded them by notching tally sticks.

In 1611, the year Cotgrave's dictionary was published, ecclesiastical court records at Sidlesham in Sussex state that two parishioners, Bartholomew Wyatt and Richard Latter, failed to attend church on Easter Sunday because they were playing cricket. They were fined 12d each and ordered to do penance.This is the earliest mention of adult participation in cricket and it was around the same time that the earliest known organised inter-parish or village match was played – at Chevening, Kent. In 1624, a player called Jasper Vinall died after he was accidentally struck on the head during a match between two parish teams in Sussex.

Cricket remained a low-key local pursuit for much of the 17th century. It is known, through numerous references found in the records of ecclesiastical court cases, to have been proscribed at times by the Puritans before and during the Commonwealth. The problem was nearly always the issue of Sunday play as the Puritans considered cricket to be "profane" if played on the Sabbath, especially if large crowds or gambling were involved.

According to the social historian Derek Birley, there was a "great upsurge of sport after the Restoration" in 1660. Gambling on sport became a problem significant enough for Parliament to pass the 1664 Gambling Act, limiting stakes to £100 which was, in any case, a colossal sum exceeding the annual income of 99% of the population. Along with prizefighting, horse racing and blood sports, cricket was perceived to be a gambling sport.Rich patrons made matches for high stakes, forming teams in which they engaged the first professional players.By the end of the century, cricket had developed into a major sport that was spreading throughout England and was already being taken abroad by English mariners and colonisers – the earliest reference to cricket overseas is dated 1676. A 1697 newspaper report survives of "a great cricket match" played in Sussex "for fifty guineas apiece" – this is the earliest known contest that is generally considered a First Class match.

- The patrons, and other players from the social class known as the "gentry", began to classify themselves as "amateurs" to establish a clear distinction from the professionals, who were invariably members of the working class, even to the point of having separate changing and dining facilities. The gentry, including such high-ranking nobles as the Dukes of Richmond, exerted their honour code of noblesse oblige to claim rights of leadership in any sporting contests they took part in, especially as it was necessary for them to play alongside their "social inferiors" if they were to win their bets. In time, a perception took hold that the typical amateur who played in first-class cricket, until 1962 when amateurism was abolished, was someone with a public school education who had then gone to one of Cambridge or Oxford University – society insisted that such people were "officers and gentlemen" whose destiny was to provide leadership. In a purely financial sense, the cricketing amateur would theoretically claim expenses for playing while his professional counterpart played under contract and was paid a wage or match fee;

in practice, many amateurs claimed more than actual expenditure and the derisive term "shamateur" was coined to describe the practice.

- **The Young Cricketer, 1768**

The game underwent major development in the 18th century to become England's national sport.Its success was underwritten by the twin necessities of patronage and betting. Cricket was prominent in London as early as 1707 and, in the middle years of the century, large crowds flocked to matches on the Artillery Ground in Finsbury. The single wicket form of the sport attracted huge crowds and wagers to match, its popularity peaking in the 1748 season. Bowling underwent an evolution around 1760 when bowlers began to pitch the ball instead of rolling or skimming it towards the batter. This caused a revolution in bat design because, to deal with the bouncing ball, it was necessary to introduce the modern straight bat in place of the old "hockey stick" shape.

The Hambledon Club was founded in the 1760s and, for the next twenty years until the formation of Marylebone Cricket Club (MCC) and the opening of Lord's Old Ground in 1787, Hambledon was both the game's greatest club and its focal point. MCC quickly became the sport's premier club and the custodian of the Laws of Cricket. New Laws introduced in the latter part of the 18th century included the three stump wicket and leg before wicket (lbw).

The 19th century saw underarm bowling superseded by first roundarm and then overarm bowling. Both developments were controversial.Organisation of the game at county level led to the creation of the county clubs, starting with Sussex in 1839. In December 1889, the eight leading county clubs formed the official County Championship, which began in 1890.

The most famous player of the 19th century was W. G. Grace, who started his long and influential career in 1865. It was especially during the career of Grace that the distinction between amateurs and professionals became blurred by the existence of players like him who were nominally amateur but, in terms of their financial gain, de facto professional. Grace himself was said to have been paid more money for playing cricket than any professional.

The last two decades before the First World War have been called the "Golden Age of cricket". It is a nostalgic name prompted by the collective sense of loss resulting from the war, but the period did produce some great players and memorable matches, especially as organised competition at county and Test level developed.

- **Cricket becomes an international sport**

In 1844, the first-ever international match took place between the United States and Canada. In 1859, a team of English players went to North America on the first overseas tour. Meanwhile, the British Empire had been instrumental in spreading the game overseas and by the middle of the 19th century it had become well established in Australia, the Caribbean, India, Pakistan, New Zealand, North America and South Africa.

In 1862, an English team made the first tour of Australia. The first Australian team to travel overseas consisted of Aboriginal stockmen who toured England in 1868. The first One Day International match was played on 5 January 1971 between Australia and England at the Melbourne Cricket Ground.

In 1876–77, an England team took part in what was retrospectively recognised as the first-ever Test match at the Melbourne Cricket Ground against Australia. The rivalry between England and Australia gave birth to The Ashes in 1882, and this has remained Test cricket's most famous contest. Test cricket began to expand in 1888–89 when South Africa played England.

- **World cricket in the 20th century**

The inter-war years were dominated by Australia's Don Bradman, statistically the greatest Test batter of all time. Test cricket continued to expand during the 20th century with the addition of the West Indies (1928), New Zealand (1930) and India (1932) before the Second World War and then Pakistan (1952), Sri Lanka (1982), Zimbabwe (1992), Bangladesh (2000), Ireland and Afghanistan (both 2018) in the post-war period. South Africa was banned from international cricket from 1970 to 1992 as part of the apartheid boycott.

- **The rise of limited overs cricket**

Cricket entered a new era in 1963 when English counties introduced the limited overs variant. As it was sure to produce a result, limited overs cricket was lucrative and the number of matches increased. The first Limited Overs International was played in 1971 and the governing International Cricket Council (ICC), seeing its potential, staged the first limited overs Cricket World Cup in 1975. In the 21st century, a new limited overs form, Twenty20, made an immediate impact. On 22 June 2017, Afghanistan and Ireland became the 11th and 12th ICC full members, enabling them to play Test cricket.

- **A typical cricket field.**

In cricket, the rules of the game are specified in a code called The Laws of Cricket (hereinafter called "the Laws") which has a global remit. There are 42 Laws (always written with a capital "L"). The earliest known version of the code was drafted in 1744 and, since 1788, it has been owned and maintained by its custodian, the Marylebone Cricket Club (MCC) in London.

- **Playing area**

Cricket is a bat-and-ball game played on a cricket field between two teams of eleven players each. The field is usually circular or oval in shape and the edge of the playing area is marked by a boundary, which may be a fence, part of the stands, a rope, a painted line or a combination of these; the boundary must if possible be marked along its entire length.

In the approximate centre of the field is a rectangular pitch (see image, below) on which a wooden target called a wicket is sited at each end; the wickets are placed 22 yards (20 m) apart. The pitch is a flat surface 10 feet (3.0 m) wide, with very short grass that tends to be worn away as the game progresses (cricket can also be played on artificial surfaces, notably matting). Each wicket is made of three wooden stumps topped by two bails.

- **Cricket pitch and creases**

As illustrated above, the pitch is marked at each end with four white painted lines: a bowling crease, a popping crease and two return creases. The three stumps are aligned centrally on the bowling crease, which is eight feet eight inches long. The popping crease is drawn four feet in front of the bowling crease and parallel to it; although it is drawn as a twelve-foot line (six feet either side of the wicket), it is, in fact, unlimited in length. The return creases are drawn at right angles to the popping crease so that they intersect the ends of the bowling crease; each return crease is drawn as an eight-foot line, so that it extends four feet behind the bowling crease, but is also, in fact, unlimited in length.

Before a match begins, the team captains (who are also players) toss a coin to decide which team will bat first and so take the first innings. Innings is the term used for each phase of play in the match.In each innings, one team bats, attempting to score runs, while the other team bowls and fields the ball, attempting to restrict the scoring and dismiss the batters. When the first innings ends, the teams change roles; there can be two to four innings depending upon the type of match. A match with four scheduled innings is played over three to five days; a match with two scheduled innings is usually completed in a single day. During an innings, all eleven members of the fielding team take the field, but usually only two members of the batting team are on the field at any given time. The exception to this is if a batter has any type of illness or injury restricting his or her ability to run, in this case the batter is allowed a runner who can run between the wickets when the batter hits a scoring run or runs,though this does not apply in international cricket. The order of batters is usually announced just before the match, but it can be varied.

The main objective of each team is to score more runs than their opponents but, in some forms of cricket, it is also necessary to dismiss all of the opposition batters in their final innings in order to win the match, which would otherwise be drawn. If the team batting last is all out having scored fewer runs than their opponents, they are said to have "lost by n runs" (where n is the difference between the aggregate number of runs scored by the teams). If the team that bats last scores enough runs to win, it is said to have "won by n wickets", where n is the number of wickets left to fall. For example, a team that passes its opponents‘ total having lost six wickets (i.e., six of their batters have been dismissed) have won the match "by four wickets".

In a two-innings-a-side match, one team's combined first and second innings total may be less than the other side's first innings total. The team with the greater score is then said to have "won by an innings and n runs", and does not need to bat again: n is the difference between the two teams' aggregate scores. If the team batting last is all out, and both sides have scored the same number of runs, then the match is a tie; this result is quite rare in matches of two innings a side with only 62 happening in first-class matches from the earliest known instance in 1741 until January 2017. In the traditional form of the game, if the time allotted for the match expires before either side can win, then the game is declared a draw.

If the match has only a single innings per side, then a maximum number of overs applies to each innings. Such a match is called a "limited overs" or "one-day" match, and the side scoring more runs wins regardless of the number of wickets lost, so that a draw cannot occur. In some cases, ties are broken by having each team bat for a one-over innings known as a Super Over; subsequent Super Overs may be played if the first Super Over ends in a tie. If this kind of match is temporarily interrupted by bad weather, then a complex mathematical formula, known as the Duckworth–Lewis–Stern method after its developers, is often used to recalculate a new target score. A one-day match can also be declared a "no-result" if fewer than a previously agreed number of overs have been bowled by either team, in circumstances that make normal resumption of play impossible; for example, wet weather.

In all forms of cricket, the umpires can abandon the match if bad light or rain makes it impossible to continue. There have been instances of entire matches, even Test matches scheduled to be played over five days, being lost to bad weather without a ball being bowled: for example, the third Test of the 1970/71 series in Australia.

- **Innings**

The innings (ending with 's' in both singular and plural form) is the term used for each phase of play during a match. Depending on the type of match being played, each team has either one or two innings. Sometimes all eleven members of the batting side take a turn to bat but, for various reasons, an innings can end before they have all done so. The innings terminates if the batting team is "all out", a term defined by the Laws: "at the fall of a wicket or the retirement of a batter, further balls remain to be bowled but no further batter is available to come in". In this situation, one of the batters has not been dismissed and is termed not out; this is because he has no partners left and there must always be two active batters while the innings is in progress.

- **An innings may end early while there are still two not out batters**

the batting team's captain may declare the innings closed even though some of his players have not had a turn to bat: this is a tactical decision by the captain, usually because he believes his team have scored sufficient runs and need time to dismiss the opposition in their innings

the set number of overs (i.e., in a limited overs match) have been bowled

the match has ended prematurely due to bad weather or running out of time

in the final innings of the match, the batting side has reached its target and won the game.

- **Overs**

The Laws state that, throughout an innings, "the ball shall be bowled from each end alternately in overs of 6 balls". The name "over" came about because the umpire calls "Over!" when six balls have been bowled. At this point, another bowler is deployed at the other end, and the fielding side changes ends while the batters do not. A bowler cannot bowl two successive overs, although a bowler can (and usually does) bowl alternate overs, from the same end, for several overs which are termed a "spell". The batters do not change ends at the end of the over, and so the one who was non-striker is now the striker and vice versa. The umpires also change positions so that the one who was at "square leg" now stands behind the wicket at the non-striker's end and vice versa.

- **Clothing and equipment**

English cricketer W. G. Grace "taking guard" in 1883. His pads and bat are very similar to those used today. The gloves have evolved somewhat. Many modern players use more defensive equipment than were available to Grace, most notably helmets and arm guards.

The wicket-keeper (a specialised fielder behind the batter) and the batters wear protective gear because of the hardness of the ball, which can be delivered at speeds of more than 145 kilometres per hour (90 mph) and presents a major health and safety concern. Protective clothing includes pads (designed to protect the knees and shins), batting gloves or wicket-keeper's gloves for the hands, a safety helmet for the head and a box for male players inside the trousers (to protect the crotch area). Some batters wear additional padding inside their shirts and trousers such as thigh pads, arm pads, rib protectors and shoulder pads. The only fielders allowed to wear protective gear are those in positions very close to the batter (i.e., if they are alongside or in front of him), but they cannot wear gloves or external leg guards.

Subject to certain variations, on-field clothing generally includes a collared shirt with short or long sleeves; long trousers; woolen pullover (if needed); cricket cap (for fielding) or a safety helmet; and spiked shoes or boots to increase traction. The kit is traditionally all white and this remains the case in Test and first-class cricket but, in limited overs cricket, team colours are worn instead.

- **Bat and ball**

Two types of cricket ball, both of the same size:

i) A used white ball. White balls are mainly used in limited overs cricket, especially in matches played at night, under floodlights (left).

ii) A used red ball. Red balls are used in Test cricket, first-class cricket and some other forms of cricket (right).

The essence of the sport is that a bowler delivers (i.e., bowls) the ball from his or her end of the pitch towards the batter who, armed with a bat, is "on strike" at the other end (see next sub-section: Basic gameplay).

The bat is made of wood, usually Salix alba (white willow), and has the shape of a blade topped by a cylindrical handle. The blade must not be more than 4.25 inches (10.8 cm) wide and the total length of the bat not more than 38 inches (97 cm). There is no standard for the weight, which is usually between 2 lb 7 oz and 3 lb (1.1 and 1.4 kg).

The ball is a hard leather-seamed spheroid, with a circumference of 9 inches (23 cm). The ball has a "seam": six rows of stitches attaching the leather shell of the ball to the string and cork interior. The seam on a new ball is prominent and helps the bowler propel it in a less predictable manner. During matches, the quality of the ball deteriorates to a point where it is no longer usable; during the course of this deterioration, its behaviour in flight will change and can influence the outcome of the match. Players will, therefore, attempt to modify the ball's behaviour by modifying its physical properties. Polishing the ball and wetting it with sweat or saliva is legal, even when the polishing is deliberately done on one side only to increase the ball's swing through the air, but the acts of rubbing other substances into the ball, scratching the surface or picking at the seam are illegal ball tampering.

- **Player roles**

Basic gameplay: bowler to batter

During normal play, thirteen players and two umpires are on the field. Two of the players are batters and the rest are all eleven members of the fielding team. The other nine players in the batting team are off the field in the pavilion. The image with overlay below shows what is happening when a ball is being bowled and which of the personnel are on or close to the pitch.

- **Return crease**

In the photo, the two batters (3 & 8; wearing yellow) have taken position at each end of the pitch (6). Three members of the fielding team (4, 10 & 11; wearing dark blue) are in shot. One of the two umpires (1; wearing white hat) is stationed behind the wicket (2) at the bowler's (4) end of the pitch. The bowler (4) is bowling the ball (5) from his end of the pitch to the batter at the other end who is called the "striker". The other batter (3) at the bowling end is called the "non-striker". The wicket-keeper (10), who is a specialist, is positioned behind the striker's wicket (9) and behind him stands one of the fielders in a position called "first slip" (11). While the bowler and the first slip are wearing conventional kit only, the two batters and the wicket-keeper are wearing protective gear including safety helmets, padded gloves and leg guards (pads).

While the umpire (1) in shot stands at the bowler's end of the pitch, his colleague stands in the outfield, usually in or near the fielding position called "square leg", so that he is in line with the popping crease (7) at the striker's end of the pitch. The bowling crease (not numbered) is the one on which the wicket is located between the return creases (12). The bowler (4) intends to hit the wicket (9) with the ball (5) or, at least, to prevent the striker (8) from scoring runs. The striker (8) intends, by using his bat, to defend his wicket and, if possible, to hit the ball away from the pitch in order to score runs.

Some players are skilled in both batting and bowling, or as either or these as well as wicket-keeping, so are termed all-rounders. Bowlers are classified according to their style, generally as fast bowlers, seam bowlers or spinners. Batters are classified according to whether they are right-handed or left-handed.

- **Fielding**

Of the eleven fielders, three are in shot in the image above. The other eight are elsewhere on the field, their positions determined on a tactical basis by the captain or the bowler. Fielders often change position between deliveries, again as directed by the captain or bowler.

If a fielder is injured or becomes ill during a match, a substitute is allowed to field instead of him, but the substitute cannot bowl or act as a captain, except in the case of concussion substitutes in international cricket. The substitute leaves the field when the injured player is fit to return. The Laws of Cricket were updated in 2017 to allow substitutes to act as wicket-keepers.

- **Bowling and dismissal**

Glenn McGrath of Australia holds the world record for most wickets in the Cricket World Cup.

Most bowlers are considered specialists in that they are selected for the team because of their skill as a bowler, although some are all-rounders and even specialist batters bowl occasionally. The specialists bowl several times during an innings but may not bowl two overs consecutively. If the captain wants a bowler to "change ends", another bowler must temporarily fill in so that the change is not immediate.

A bowler reaches his delivery stride by means of a "run-up" and an over is deemed to have begun when the bowler starts his run-up for the first delivery of that over, the ball then being "in play".

Fast bowlers, needing momentum, take a lengthy run up while bowlers with a slow delivery take no more than a couple of steps before bowling. The fastest bowlers can deliver the ball at a speed of over 145 kilometres per hour (90 mph) and they sometimes rely on sheer speed to try to defeat the batter, who is forced to react very quickly.

Other fast bowlers rely on a mixture of speed and guile by making the ball seam or swing (i.e. curve) in flight. This type of delivery can deceive a batter into miscuing his shot, for example, so that the ball just touches the edge of the bat and can then be "caught behind" by the wicket-keeper or a slip fielder. At the other end of the bowling scale is the spin bowler who bowls at a relatively slow pace and relies entirely on guile to deceive the batter. A spinner will often "buy his wicket" by "tossing one up" (in a slower, steeper parabolic path) to lure the batter into making a poor shot. The batter has to be very wary of such deliveries as they are often "flighted" or spun so that the ball will not behave quite as he expects and he could be "trapped" into getting himself out. In between the pacemen and the spinners are the medium paced seamers who rely on persistent accuracy to try to contain the rate of scoring and wear down the batter's concentration.

There are nine ways in which a batter can be dismissed: five relatively common and four extremely rare. The common forms of dismissal are bowled, caught, leg before wicket (lbw), run out and stumped. Rare methods are hit wicket,hit the ball twice, obstructing the field and timed out. The Laws state that the fielding team, usually the bowler in practice, must appeal for a dismissal before the umpire can give his decision. If the batter is out, the umpire raises a forefinger and says "Out!"; otherwise, he will shake his head and say "Not out".There is, effectively, a tenth method of dismissal, retired out, which is not an on-field dismissal as such but rather a retrospective one for which no fielder is credited.

- **Batting, runs and extras**

The directions in which a right-handed batter, facing down the page, intends to send the ball when playing various cricketing shots. The diagram for a left-handed batter is a mirror image of this one.

Batters take turns to bat via a batting order which is decided beforehand by the team captain and presented to the umpires, though the order remains flexible when the captain officially nominates the team. Substitute batters are generally not allowed, except in the case of concussion substitutes in international cricket.

In order to begin batting the batter first adopts a batting stance. Standardly, this involves adopting a slight crouch with the feet pointing across the front of the wicket, looking in the direction of the bowler, and holding the bat so it passes over the feet and so its tip can rest on the ground near to the toes of the back foot.

A skilled batter can use a wide array of "shots" or "strokes" in both defensive and attacking mode. The idea is to hit the ball to the best effect with the flat surface of the bat's blade. If the ball touches the side of the bat it is called an "edge". The batter does not have to play a shot and can allow the ball to go through to the wicketkeeper. Equally, he does not have to attempt a run when he hits the ball with his bat. Batters do not always seek to hit the ball as hard as possible, and a good player can score runs just by making a deft stroke with a turn of the wrists or by simply "blocking" the ball but directing it away from fielders so that he has time to take a run. A wide variety of shots are played, the batter's repertoire including strokes named according to the style of swing and the direction aimed: e.g., "cut", "drive", "hook", "pull".

The batter on strike (i.e. the "striker") must prevent the ball hitting the wicket, and try to score runs by hitting the ball with his bat so that he and his partner have time to run from one end of the pitch to the other before the fielding side can return the ball. To register a run, both runners must touch the ground behind the popping crease with either their bats or their bodies (the batters carry their bats as they run). Each completed run increments the score of both the team and the striker.

- **Sachin Tendulkar is the only player to have scored one hundred international centuries**

The decision to attempt a run is ideally made by the batter who has the better view of the ball's progress, and this is communicated by calling: usually "yes", "no" or "wait". More than one run can be scored from a single hit: hits worth one to three runs are common, but the size of the field is such that it is usually difficult to run four or more. To compensate for this, hits that reach the boundary of the field are automatically awarded four runs if the ball touches the ground en route to the boundary or six runs if the ball clears the boundary without touching the ground within the boundary. In these cases the batters do not need to run. Hits for five are unusual and generally rely on the help of "overthrows" by a fielder returning the ball. If an odd number of runs is scored by the striker, the two batters have changed ends, and the one who was non-striker is now the striker. Only the striker can score individual runs, but all runs are added to the team's total.

Additional runs can be gained by the batting team as extras (called "sundries" in Australia) due to errors made by the fielding side. This is achieved in four ways: no-ball, a penalty of one extra conceded by the bowler if he breaks the rules; wide, a penalty of one extra conceded by the bowler if he bowls so that the ball is out of the batter's reach bye, an extra awarded if the batter misses the ball and it goes past the wicket-keeper and gives the batters time to run in the conventional way leg bye, as for a bye except that the ball has hit the batter's body, though not his bat. If the bowler has conceded a no-ball or a wide, his team incurs an additional penalty because that ball (i.e., delivery) has to be bowled again and hence the batting side has the opportunity to score more runs from this extra ball.

- **Specialist roles**

Captain (cricket) and Wicket-keeper

The captain is often the most experienced player in the team, certainly the most tactically astute, and can possess any of the main skillsets as a batter, a bowler or a wicket-keeper. Within the Laws, the captain has certain responsibilities in terms of nominating his players to the umpires before the match and ensuring that his players conduct themselves "within the spirit and traditions of the game as well as within the Laws".

The wicket-keeper (sometimes called simply the "keeper") is a specialist fielder subject to various rules within the Laws about his equipment and demeanour. He is the only member of the fielding side who can effect a stumping and is the only one permitted to wear gloves and external leg guards. Depending on their primary skills, the other ten players in the team tend to be classified as specialist batters or specialist bowlers. Generally, a team will include five or six specialist batters and four or five specialist bowlers, plus the wicket-keeper.

- **Umpires and scorers**

The game on the field is regulated by the two umpires, one of whom stands behind the wicket at the bowler's end, the other in a position called "square leg" which is about 15–20 metres away from the batter on strike and in line with the popping crease on which he is taking guard. The umpires have several responsibilities including adjudication on whether a ball has been correctly bowled (i.e., not a no-ball or a wide); when a run is scored; whether a batter is out (the fielding side must first appeal to the umpire, usually with the phrase "How's that?" or "Owzat?"); when intervals start and end; and the suitability of the pitch, field and weather for playing the game. The umpires are authorised to interrupt or even abandon a match due to circumstances likely to endanger the players, such as a damp pitch or deterioration of the light.

Off the field in televised matches, there is usually a third umpire who can make decisions on certain incidents with the aid of video evidence. The third umpire is mandatory under the playing conditions for Test and Limited Overs

International matches played between two ICC full member countries. These matches also have a match referee whose job is to ensure that play is within the Laws and the spirit of the game.

The match details, including runs and dismissals, are recorded by two official scorers, one representing each team. The scorers are directed by the hand signals of an umpire . For example, the umpire raises a forefinger to signal that the batter is out (has been dismissed); he raises both arms above his head if the batter has hit the ball for six runs. The scorers are required by the Laws to record all runs scored, wickets taken and overs bowled; in practice, they also note significant amounts of additional data relating to the game.

A match's statistics are summarised on a scorecard. Prior to the popularisation of scorecards, most scoring was done by men sitting on vantage points cuttings notches on tally sticks and runs were originally called notches.According to Rowland Bowen, the earliest known scorecard templates were introduced in 1776 by T. Pratt of Sevenoaks and soon came into general use.It is believed that scorecards were printed and sold at Lord's for the first time in 1846.

FOUR

HISTORY OF CRICKET

- **History of cricket**

The sport of cricket has a known history beginning in the late 16th century. Having originated in south-east England, it became an established sport in the country in the 18th century and developed globally in the 19th and 20th centuries. International matches have been played since the 19th-century and formal Test cricket matches are considered to date from 1877. Cricket is the world's second most popular spectator sport after association football (soccer).

Internationally, cricket is governed by the International Cricket Council (ICC) which has over one hundred countries and territories in membership although only twelve currently play Test cricket.

- **Origin**

Cricket was probably created during Saxon or Norman times by children living in the Weald, an area of dense woodlands and clearings in south-east England that lies across Kent and Sussex. The first definite written reference is from the end of the 16th-century.

There have been several speculations about the game's origins, including some that it was created in France or Flanders. The earliest of these speculative references is from 1300 and concerns the future King Edward II playing at "creag and other games" in both Westminster and Newenden. It has been suggested that "creag" was an Old English word for cricket, but expert opinion is that it was an early spelling of "craic", meaning "fun and games in general".

It is generally believed that cricket survived as a children's game for many generations before it was increasingly taken up by adults around the beginning of the 17th century. Possibly cricket was derived from bowls, assuming bowls is the older sport, by the intervention of a batsman trying to stop the ball from reaching its target by hitting it away. Playing on sheep-grazed land or in clearings, the original implements may have been a matted lump of sheep's wool (or even a stone or a small lump of wood) as the ball; a stick or a crook or another farm tool as the bat; and a stool or a tree stump or a gate (e.g., a wicket gate) as the wicket.

- **First definite reference**

John Derrick was a pupil at the Royal Grammar School, then the Free School, in Guildford when he and his friends played creckett circa 1550.

In 1597 (Old Style – 1598 New Style) a court case in England concerning an ownership dispute over a plot of common land in Guildford, Surrey, mentions the game of creckett. A 59-year-old coroner, John Derrick, testified that he and his school friends had played creckett on the site fifty years earlier when they attended the Free School. Derrick's account proves beyond reasonable doubt that the game was being played in Surrey circa 1550, and is the earliest universally accepted reference to the game.

The first reference to cricket being played as an adult sport was in 1611, when two men in Sussex were prosecuted for playing cricket on Sunday instead of going to church. In the same year, a dictionary defined cricket as a boys' game, and this suggests that adult participation was a recent development.

- **Derivation of the name of "cricket"**

A number of words are thought to be possible sources for the term "cricket". In the earliest definite reference, it was spelled creckett. The name may have been derived from the Middle Dutch krick(-e), meaning a stick; or the Old English cricc or cryce meaning a crutch or staff, or the French word criquet meaning a wooden post. The Middle Dutch word krickstoel means a long low stool used for kneeling in church; this resembled the long low wicket with two stumps used in early cricket. According to Heiner Gillmeister, a European language expert of the University of Bonn, "cricket" derives from the Middle Dutch phrase for hockey, met de (krik ket)sen (i.e., "with the stick chase").

It is more likely that the terminology of cricket was based on words in use in south-east England at the time and, given trade connections with the County of Flanders, especially in the 15th century when it belonged to the Duchy of Burgundy, many Middle Dutch words found their way into southern English dialects.

- **The Commonwealth**

After the Civil War ended in 1648, the new Puritan government clamped down on "unlawful assemblies", in particular the more raucous sports such as football. Their laws also demanded a stricter observance of the Sabbath than there had been previously. As the Sabbath was the only free time available to the lower classes, cricket's popularity may have waned during the Commonwealth. However, it did flourish in public fee-paying schools such as Winchester and St Paul's. There is no actual evidence that Oliver Cromwell's regime banned cricket specifically and there are references to it during the interregnum that suggest it was acceptable to the authorities provided that it did not cause any "breach of the Sabbath". It is believed that the nobility in general adopted cricket at this time through involvement in village games.

- **Gambling and press coverage**

Cricket thrived after the Restoration in 1660 and is believed to have first attracted gamblers making large bets at this time. It is possible, as believed by some historians, that top-class matches began. In 1664, the "Cavalier" Parliament passed the Gaming Act 1664 which limited stakes to £100, although that was still a fortune at the time, equivalent to about £16,000 in present-day terms. Cricket had become a significant gambling sport by the end of the 17th century, as evidenced in 1697 by a newspaper report of a "great match" played in Sussex which was 11-a-side and played for high stakes of 50 guineas a side.

With freedom of the press having been granted in 1696, cricket for the first time could be reported in the newspapers. But it was a long time before the newspaper industry adapted sufficiently to provide frequent, let alone comprehensive, coverage of the game. During the first half of the 18th century, press reports tended to focus on the betting rather than on the play.

- **18th-century cricket**

Gambling introduced the first patrons because some of the gamblers decided to strengthen their bets by forming their own teams and it is believed the first "county teams" were formed in the aftermath of the Restoration in 1660, especially as members of the nobility were employing "local experts" from village cricket as the earliest professionals. The first known game in which the teams use county names is in 1709 but there can be little doubt that these sort of fixtures were being arranged long before that. The match in 1697 was probably Sussex versus another county.

The most notable of the early patrons were a group of aristocrats and businessmen who were active from about 1725, which is the time that press coverage became more regular, perhaps as a result of the patrons' influence. These men included the 2nd Duke of Richmond, Sir William Gage, Alan Brodrick and Edwin Stead. For the first time, the press mentions individual players like Thomas Waymark.

- **Cricket expands beyond England**

Cricket was introduced to North America via the English colonies in the 17th century, probably before it had even reached the north of England. In the 18th century it arrived in other parts of the globe. It was introduced to the West Indies by colonists and to India by East India Company mariners in the first half of the century. It arrived in Australia almost as soon as colonisation began in 1788. New Zealand and South Africa followed in the early years of the 19th century.

Cricket never caught on in Canada, despite efforts by the upper class to promote the game as a way of identifying with the "mother country". Canada, unlike Australia and the West Indies, witnessed a continual decline in the popularity of the game during 1860 to 1960. Linked in the public consciousness to an upper-class sport, the game never became popular with the general public. In the summer season it had to compete with baseball. During the First World War, Canadian units stationed in France played baseball instead of cricket.

- **Development Laws of Cricket**

It's not clear when the basic rules of cricket such as bat and ball, the wicket, pitch dimensions, overs, how out, etc. were originally formulated. In 1728, the Duke of Richmond and Alan Brodick drew up Articles of Agreement to determine the code of practice in a particular game and this became a common feature, especially around payment of stake money and distributing the winnings given the importance of gambling.

In 1744, the Laws of Cricket were codified for the first time and then amended in 1774, when innovations such as lbw, middle stump and maximum bat width were added.

These laws stated that "the principals shall choose from amongst the gentlemen present two umpires who shall absolutely decide all disputes". The codes were drawn up by the so-called "Star and Garter Club" whose members ultimately founded the Marylebone Cricket Club at Lord's in 1787. The MCC immediately became the custodian of the Laws and has made periodic revisions and recodifications subsequently.

- **Continued growth in England**

The game continued to spread throughout England, and, in 1751, Yorkshire is first mentioned as a venue. The original form of bowling (i.e., rolling the ball along the ground as in bowls) was superseded sometime after 1760 when bowlers began to pitch the ball and study variations in line, length and pace. Scorecards began to be kept on a regular basis from 1772; since then, an increasingly clear picture has emerged of the sport's development.

- **An artwork depicting the history of the cricket bat**

The first famous clubs were London and Dartford in the early 18th century. London played its matches on the Artillery Ground, which still exists. Others followed, particularly Slindon in Sussex, which was backed by the Duke of Richmond and featured the star player Richard Newland. There were other prominent clubs at Maidenhead, Hornchurch, Maidstone, Sevenoaks, Bromley, Addington, Hadlow and Chertsey.

But far and away the most famous of the early clubs was Hambledon in Hampshire. It started as a parish organisation that first achieved prominence in 1756. The club itself was founded in the 1760s and was well patronised to the extent that it was the focal point of the game for about thirty years until the formation of MCC and the opening of Lord's Cricket Ground in 1787. Hambledon produced several outstanding players including the master batsman John Small and the first great fast bowler Thomas Brett. Their most notable opponent was the Chertsey and Surrey bowler Edward "Lumpy" Stevens, who is believed to have been the main proponent of the flighted delivery.

It was in answer to the flighted, or pitched, delivery that the straight bat was introduced. The old "hockey stick"–style of bat was only really effective against the ball being trundled or skimmed along the ground. First-class cricket began, retrospectively, in 1772.A Game of Cricket at The Royal Academy Club in Marylebone Fields, now Regent's Park, depiction by unknown artist, c. 1790–1799

- **History of cricket (1772–1815) and History of English cricket (1816–1863)**

The game also underwent a fundamental change of organisation with the formation for the first time of county clubs. All the modern county clubs, starting with Sussex in 1839, were founded during the 19th century. No sooner had the first county clubs established themselves than they faced what amounted to "player action" as William Clarke created the travelling All-England Eleven in 1846. Though a commercial venture, this team did much to popularise the game in districts which had never previously been visited by high-class cricketers. Other similar teams were created and this vogue lasted for about thirty years. But the counties and MCC prevailed.

- **A cricket match at Darnall, Sheffield in the 1820s.**

The growth of cricket in the mid and late 19th century was assisted by the development of the railway network. For the first time, teams from a long distance apart could play one other without a prohibitively time-consuming journey. Spectators could travel longer distances to matches, increasing the size of crowds. Army units around the Empire had time on their hands, and encouraged the locals so they could have some entertaining competition. Most of the Empire embraced cricket, with the exception of Canada.

In 1864, another bowling revolution resulted in the legalisation of overarm and in the same year. W. G. Grace began his long and influential career at this time, his feats doing much to increase cricket's popularity. He introduced technical innovations which revolutionised the game, particularly in batting.

- **International cricket begins**

The first ever international cricket game was between the US and Canada in 1844. The match was played at the grounds of the St George's Cricket Club in New York.

- **The English team 1859 on their way to the US**

In 1859, a team of leading English professionals set off to North America on the first-ever overseas tour and, in 1862, the first English team toured Australia. Between May and October 1868, a team of Aboriginal Australians toured England in what was the first Australian cricket team to travel overseas.

- **The first Australian touring team (1878) pictured at Niagara Falls**

In 1877, an England touring team in Australia played two matches against full Australian XIs that are now regarded as the inaugural Test matches. The following year, the Australians toured England for the first time and the success of this tour ensured a popular demand for similar ventures in future. No Tests were played in 1878 but more soon followed and, at The Oval in 1882, the Australian victory in a tense finish gave rise to The Ashes.South Africa became the third Test nation in 1889.

- **National championships**

A significant development in domestic cricket occurred in 1890 when the official County Championship was constituted in England. Soon afterwards, in May 1894, the sport's first-class standard was officially defined. This organisational initiative has been repeated in other countries. Australia established the Sheffield Shield in 1892–93. Other national competitions to be established were the Currie Cup in South Africa, the Plunket Shield in New Zealand and the Ranji Trophy in India. The ICC re-defined first-class status in 1947 as a global concept.

The period from 1890 to the outbreak of the First World War has become one of nostalgia, ostensibly because the teams played cricket according to "the spirit of the game", but more realistically because it was a peacetime period that was shattered by the First World War. The era has been called The Golden Age of cricket and it featured numerous great names such as Grace, Wilfred Rhodes, C. B. Fry, Ranjitsinhji and Victor Trumper.

- **Balls per over**

During most of the 19th-century standard overs were made up of four deliveries. In 1889 five-ball overs were introduced in first-class cricket, with a move to generally use six-ball overs in 1900.

In the 20th-century, eight-ball overs were used at times in a number of countries, primarily Australia, where eight-balls were the standard over length between 1918/19 and 1978/79, South Africa and New Zealand. Since the 1979/80 Australian and New Zealand seasons, six balls per over have been used worldwide, and the most recent version of the Laws only permits six-ball overs.

- **Growth of international cricket**

Sid Barnes traps Lala Amarnath lbw in the first official Test between Australia and India at the MCG in 1948

The Imperial Cricket Conference was founded in 1909 with England, Australia and South Africa as the founder members. This aimed to regulate international cricket between the three sides, considered the only three of equal status at the time. West Indies were admitted as members in 1928, allowing them to play Test cricket against the other sides. New Zealand and India both became Test playing nations before World War II and Pakistan joined soon afterwards in 1952.

At the initial suggestion of Pakistan, the ICC was expanded to include non-Test playing countries from 1965, with Associate members being admitted. At the same time the organisation changed its name to the International Cricket Conference. The first limited-overs World Cups were played during the 1970s and Sri Lanka became the first

Associate member to be raised to Test playing status in 1982.

The international game continued to grow with the introduction of Affiliate Member status in 1984, a level of membership designed for sides with less history of playing cricket. In 1989 the ICC renamed itself the International Cricket Council. Zimbabwe became Full Members in 1992 and Bangladesh in 2000 before Afghanistan and Ireland were both admitted as Test sides in 2018, bringing the number of full members of the ICC to 12.

- **International cricket in South Africa from 1971 to 1981**

The greatest crisis to hit international cricket was brought about by apartheid, the South African policy of racial segregation. The situation began to crystallise after 1961 when South Africa left the Commonwealth of Nations and so, under the rules of the day, its cricket board had to leave the International Cricket Conference (ICC). Cricket's opposition to apartheid intensified in 1968 with the cancellation of England's tour to South Africa by the South African authorities, due to the inclusion in the England team of Basil D'Oliveira, a Cape Coloured player. In 1970, the ICC members voted to suspend South Africa indefinitely from international cricket competition.

Starved of top-level competition for its best players, the South African Cricket Board began funding so-called "rebel tours", offering large sums of money for international players to form teams and tour South Africa. The ICC's response was to blacklist any rebel players who agreed to tour South Africa, banning them from officially sanctioned international cricket. As players were poorly remunerated during the 1970s, several accepted the offer to tour South Africa, particularly players getting towards the end of their careers for which a blacklisting would have little effect.

The rebel tours continued into the 1980s but then progress was made in South African politics and it became clear that apartheid was ending. South Africa, now a "Rainbow Nation" under Nelson Mandela, was welcomed back into international sport in 1991.

- **World Series Cricket**

The money problems of top cricketers were also the root cause of another cricketing crisis that arose in 1977 when the Australian media magnate Kerry Packer fell out with the Australian Cricket Board over TV rights. Taking advantage of the low remuneration paid to players, Packer retaliated by signing several of the best players in the world to a privately run cricket league outside the structure of international cricket. World Series Cricket hired some of the banned South African players and allowed them to show off their skills in an international arena against other world-class players. The schism lasted only until 1979 and the "rebel" players were allowed back into established international cricket, though many found that their national teams had moved on without them. Long-term results of World Series Cricket have included the introduction of significantly higher player salaries and innovations such as coloured kit and night games.

- **Limited-overs cricket**

In the 1960s, English county teams began playing a version of cricket with games of only one innings each and a maximum number of overs per innings. Starting in 1963 as a knockout competition only, limited-overs cricket grew in popularity and, in 1969, a national league was created which consequently caused a reduction in the number of matches in the County Championship. The status of limited overs matches is governed by the official List A categorisation. Although many "traditional" cricket fans objected to the shorter form of the game, limited-overs cricket did have the advantage of delivering a result to spectators within a single day; it did improve cricket's appeal to younger or busier people; and it did prove commercially successful.

The first limited-overs international match took place at Melbourne Cricket Ground in 1971 as a time-filler after a Test match had been abandoned because of heavy rain on the opening days. It was tried simply as an experiment and to give the players some exercise, but turned out to be immensely popular. limited-overs internationals (LOIs or ODIs—one-day internationals) have since grown to become a massively popular form of the game, especially for busy people who want to be able to see a whole match. The International Cricket Council reacted to this development by organising the first Cricket World Cup in England in 1975, with all the Test-playing nations taking part.

- **Analytic and graphic technology**

Limited-overs cricket increased television ratings for cricket coverage. Innovative techniques introduced in coverage of limited-over matches were soon adopted for Test coverage. The innovations included presentation of in-depth statistics and graphical analysis, placing miniature cameras in the stumps, multiple usage of cameras to provide shots from several locations around the ground, high-speed photography and computer graphics technology enabling television viewers to study the course of a delivery and help them understand an umpire's decision.

In 1992, the use of a third umpire to adjudicate run-out appeals with television replays was introduced in the Test series between South Africa and India. The third umpire's duties have subsequently expanded to include decisions on other aspects of play such as stumpings, catches and boundaries. From 2011, the third umpire was being called upon to moderate review of umpires' decisions, including lbw, with the aid of virtual-reality tracking technologies (e.g., Hawk-Eye and Hot Spot), though such measures still could not free some disputed decisions from heated controversy.

- **21st-century cricket**

In June 2001, the ICC introduced a "Test Championship Table" and, in October 2002, a "One-day International Championship Table". As indicated by ICC rankings, the various cricket formats have continued to be a major competitive sport in most former British Empire countries, notably the Indian subcontinent, and new participants including the Netherlands. In 2017, the number of countries with full ICC membership was increased to twelve by the addition of Afghanistan and Ireland.

The ICC expanded its development programme, aiming to produce more national teams capable of competing at the various formats. Development efforts are focused on African and Asian nations, and on the United States. In 2004, the ICC Intercontinental Cup brought first-class cricket to 12 nations, mostly for the first time. Cricket's newest innovation is Twenty20, essentially an evening entertainment. It has so far enjoyed enormous popularity and has attracted large attendances at matches as well as good TV audience ratings. The inaugural ICC Twenty20 World Cup tournament was held in 2007. The formation of Twenty20 leagues in India – the unofficial Indian Cricket League, which started in 2007, and the official Indian Premier League, starting in 2008 – raised much speculation in the cricketing press about their effect on the future of cricket.

Thank You

Thank You For Reading This Book And Shared This Book To Friends As Birthday Gift Have A Wonderfull Day .

9 798889 235491

Printed by Libri Plureos GmbH in Hamburg,
Germany